WHAT TO DO
WHEN A LOVED ONE DIES
OR BECOMES INCAPACITATED

A COMPREHENSIVE INSTRUCTION MANUAL FOR EXECUTORS
AND SUCCESSOR TRUSTEES IN THE EVENT OF THE
INCAPACITY OR DEATH OF A LOVED ONE

Robert D. Vale
Stefani C. Coggins
Brett S. Lytle

I

DEDICATION

This handbook was created by Robert D. Vale, Stefani C. Coggins, and Brett S. Lytle, with the help and advice of our extensive legal community and the experience gained by working with our varied clients through the estate administration process. It is a work of collaboration that represents the values and practices that have been instilled in the firm since 1953. At McDowall Cotter, APC, we strive to continue achieving the same level of excellence and legal services that our founders have provided before us.

CONTENTS

INTRODUCTION TO THE ROLES- WHAT HAVE I GOTTEN MYSELF INTO?

CHAPTER ONE
THE DIFFERENCE BETWEEN TRUSTEES AND EXECUTORS

TRUSTEE, EXECUTOR- WHAT'S THE DIFFERENCE?

Both Trustees and Executors are *"Fiduciaries"*. You will hear a lot more about fiduciaries and their roles later. For now, know that you are assuming significant responsibilities once you accept the role of either Trustee or Executor.

Most folks serving as a *fiduciary* consider themselves to be *Executors*. Most of the time they are actually serving as *Trustees*. The difference is significant.

If you are an *Executor*, the estate owned by the decedent is going through a PROBATE process, most likely because the decedent died with only a Will. If the decedent died with no estate plan, then the State of California gives the decedent a Will and the Executor in that case is referred to as an Administrator.

If you are a *Trustee*, you are operating under the terms of a Revocable Living Trust, and you are operating outside of the court system, at least for the most part.

That is a BIG difference! This manual addresses the roles of both Executors and Trustees.

INCAPACITY VERSUS DEATH

A Revocable *Living* Trust is just that, it is a living document. It is effective the date it is signed by its maker. A *Will* is not a living document. While it is signed today, it does not speak until its maker dies.

An individual named to serve as a *Successor Trustee* may serve in that position if the maker(s) of the trust is *incapacitated* or *dead*. By the way, when we refer to "incapacitated", we are referring to an individual who cannot manage his or her daily *financial* affairs. So, a person with a broken leg might be physically disabled for a period of time, but that person will most likely still have the capacity to manage his or her financial affairs. However, a person who suffered a stroke or who is in the advanced stages of dementia may well be unable to manage his or her financial affairs and thus be *"incapacitated".*

An Executor named in the Will can serve as Executor *only upon the death* of the maker of the Will. Simply put, a Will does not provide for incapacity planning, it addresses only death planning.

We will discuss the role of incapacity Trustee in this manual. With a Will, unless there is a Financial Power of Attorney, incapacity planning is conducted through the court system through a "conservatorship". While appropriate in certain instances, the conservatorship process is complex, time consuming and expensive. The conservatorship process is beyond the scope of this manual. What you want to know is that conservatorships are to be avoided for the most part, as conservatorships are time consuming, expensive, and intrusive.

As you can appreciate, the role of a Trustee serving for an incapacitated individual is typically a much more difficult role, or at least a more involved role than the role of death Trustee. This is because you not only have all of the regular duties of a death Trustee, you need to deal with the ongoing financial obligations of the incapacitated individual or be in communication with the person performing that role.

This manual will first address the role of Trustee, at both incapacity and death. In a later chapter, the manual will generally address the role of Executor in the Probate setting.

CHAPTER TWO
I AM THE TRUSTEE—WHAT DO I DO NOW?

Estate administration can be a complex and often emotional undertaking. A loved one – your spouse, parent, sibling, friend – has become incapacitated or died. You are named as the Trustee and you are being asked to administer the estate of the loved one.

This manual is not intended to eliminate your need to work with an attorney in administering the estate- we strongly encourage you to do so as there are many rules and traps for the unwary and, as you will see, your responsibilities are significant and many. However, this manual should help to orient you to the tasks of a Trustee, answer some of your questions, and help you gather the information and documentation we will need to help you fulfill your duties as the appointed *fiduciary*.

Now that you have learned that you have been, or will be, appointed to serve as a Trustee, you have opened this book wondering what the heck you have got yourself into. Here are some initial FAQ's to get you started.

What do you mean, I just took on a huge responsibility?

Imagine a plow horse in a cold, dusty field, pulling a plow though hard ground as the farmer whips and screams at him. The plow horse works hard all day and gets no credit from the farmer for his labors. If the plowed line is not straight, the plow horse is berated by the farmer and put away in the stable for the night without hay.

Now imagine- you are that plow horse- Congratulations Trustee!

How did I get into this predicament?

You are serving as Trustee because someone **trusted** you and had confidence in your ability to serve as the overseer of their finances in the event of incapacity or death. You may be serving alone as a sole Trustee, or you may be serving as a co-Trustee with one or two other persons or as co-Trustee with a bank's Trust Department.

What is a Trustee and what do I do as Trustee?

The rest of the first portion of this guide is devoted to providing you with a comprehensive explanation of your duties and respon-sibilities as Trustee. Here is what we can tell you initially:

By agreeing to serve as Trustee, you have taken on a **JOB**. Whether or not you request compensation for your services as Trustee, as a Trustee you are charged with duties and responsibilities that you are required to perform in a reasonably competent and timely manner. That is pretty much the definition of a JOB.

You are a **FIDUCIARY**. You are charged with the same level of care to the beneficiaries that an attorney owes his or her clients and that a banker owes his or her customers. It is the highest, most rigorous duty imposed under California law. So, in your new JOB, you have very small margins for error, and if you go outside those margins you will breach your fiduciary duty to the beneficiaries and face potential *personal liability*. As you are starting to appreciate, your new JOB is not to be taken lightly.

HOW IS THIS THING GOING TO GO FOR ME?

How difficult or less difficult your Trustee tenure will be depends on many things, some of which you have no control over. Some of the factors are:

- Is the trust-based estate plan you are working under complete and updated?

- Are the terms of the Revocable Living Trust clear?

- Are the assets that are supposed to be in the trust actually titled in the name of the trust?

- If there are multiple beneficiaries how well did they get along with decedent and how well do they get along with each other? Family squabbles, particularly between siblings, can grow bitter and present significant problems for you as the Trustee during the time of your service, particularly if you are the Trustee and a beneficiary.

Fundamental Propositions you should memorize now

This manual provides a blow by blow instruction handbook for Trustees. However, from a 5-miles-up perspective, your fundamental duties include:

1. The requirement to account for every penny of the money you are managing. If you cannot account for money, you may have to pay it back to the trust **from your own pocket!**

2. The requirement to report to the beneficiaries *early and often.*

3. The requirement to treat the beneficiaries (including yourself, if you are a beneficiary) *equally-* you cannot favor one beneficiary over the other.

4. The requirement to follow the terms of the trust instrument that named you as Trustee. *Read the trust.*

CHAPTER THREE
YOUR DUTIES AS TRUSTEE

Fiduciary duties as Trustee

Remember that **your fiduciary duties come first** any time you act in your capacity as Trustee. In order for you to have a good feel for your duties, you need to understand what a trust is.

A **trust is a legal contract/relationship** that results when a person (often called a *trustmaker, trustor, settlor,* or *grantor*) makes a contract/agreement with a *Trustee* to handle property for the benefit of the *beneficiaries.* The agreement is normally set out in a written document, which is called the *trust instrument, declaration of trust* or the *trust agreement.* Your first and foremost duty as a Trustee is to read, understand, and faithfully follow the terms, which means instructions, of the trust instrument.

Once the trust agreement is made, the Trustmaker transfers property to the Trustee. The Trustee actually becomes the *legal* owner of the property. However, the "real" owners of the property are the beneficiaries, who are said to be the *equitable* or *beneficial* owners; they are the ones who are supposed to benefit from the property. When the Trustmaker becomes incapacitated or dies, the successor Trustee(s) named in the trust becomes the Trustee(s). Upon the death of the Trustmaker, the successor Trustee(s) holds the assets of the trust for the benefit of the beneficiaries named in the trust.

A trust can have more than one Trustee at a time. Each *co-Trustee* must decide for himself or herself how best to carry out his or her fiduciary duties. Beware that a co-Trustee **can be held responsible for another co-Trustee's breach** of a fiduciary duty. Thus, it is important that all co-Trustees **pay close attention** to everything that is done in the administration of the trust. If there is any question or problem, that should be communicated to the other co-Trustee or co-Trustees immediately. As a general rule, where there are two co-Trustees both have to agree on all matters of trust administration, and where there are three or more co-Trustees the majority rules, unless the trust instructions say something else. In order to minimize the chances of being held responsible for someone else's poor judgment or breach of duty, a co-Trustee should be sure to **make a written record** of any points of disagreement about trust business. In extreme cases, a co-Trustee **may be required to blow the whistle** on the activities of the other co-Trustee(s).

If you ever have questions about what to do as Trustee, you should **seek appropriate advice** immediately. You should not hesitate to consult your attorney, your accountant, or other trusted advisors.

The fact that you have been named as a successor Trustee in someone's trust instrument does not obligate you to accept that position. You must **consider your decision** to accept the job of Trustee very carefully. Once you accept the position, you accept all that goes with it. It is a position of **great honor**, and it involves

great responsibility and **liability.** This is not a position to accept lightly.

FUNDAMENTAL DUTIES AS A TRUSTEE

Trustees are subject to a variety of duties, some of which are summarized below. **Please bear in mind that the penalty for your breaching any of these duties is that you will have to pay for any resulting damage to the trust out of your own pocket. Personal liability—even if you are not paid for your efforts—is one of the things that goes along with being a fiduciary.**

Duty of general prudence

You, as Trustee, are duty bound to deal with the trust property as a "prudent person" would deal with the property of another. Note that this is a standard of conduct rather than of performance. Your actions (or times of inaction) will be judged against what a reasonable person would have done in the same circumstances, given the same limitations to which you were subject, and armed with the same information that was at your disposal. If you conduct yourself properly, you will not be faulted if something bad happens, such as a decline in the value of trust assets. Acting reasonably in the circumstances is your basic job description, and if you do that, you generally need not worry about being judged in the light of hindsight. Note that if you have—or claim to have—special expertise in connection with any facet of trust administration, you will be duty bound to exercise that expertise. Thus, the standard for judging your job performance will take into account your special abilities (whether actual or claimed).

Duty to carry out the terms of the trust

One noted authority states: "the first and most important duty of the Trustee is to study and become thoroughly familiar with the provisions of the trust instrument, and thereafter to follow them out implicitly." Loring, *A Trustee's Handbook* (Rounds 2002 ed.), p. 12. It will be difficult for anyone to find fault with the performance of your fiduciary duties if everything you do is in accordance with the terms of the trust instrument. If at any time you are reasonably in doubt as to the correct interpretation of the trust instrument, you will be able to petition a court for instructions and should do so.

Duty of loyalty

As a Trustee, you must always act to further the interests of the trust and the beneficiaries. You are serving as Trustee for the benefit of someone other than yourself. You should not enter into a transaction that gives you an opportunity to benefit yourself at all, much less at the expense of the trust. If any situation should arise in which there is a conflict between your personal interests and the trust, or between the trust and the interests of third parties, you as Trustee should put the interests of the trust first. For example, you should not sell trust property to yourself, or sell your property to the trust, because this creates the appearance that you may have taken advantage of the trust. Similarly, you should never loan trust funds to yourself. The rules set forth in this paragraph are strictly applied not only to transactions in which you deal directly with yourself, but also to transactions in which you deal with entities (such as partnerships or corporations) in which you are personally interested. These rules apply even though a particular transaction may be scrupulously fair, and even if it is advantageous to the trust.

Please note that California law allows you to obtain a court's permission to enter into a transaction between yourself and the trust. Thus, the only way to take this action is to petition the court for instruction and disclose everything to the court and let the judge make the decision. This will require notifying all of the beneficiaries of the proposed transaction and giving them the opportunity take positions before the court as to why the transaction should or should not be allowed to go forward. The fact that the law gives you this opportunity means that you will be judged very harshly if you ever do enter into a transaction involving a conflict of interest without prior court permission.

Duty not to delegate

Once you have accepted the position of Trustee, you are responsible for the administration of the trust, and you should not turn over the complete administration of the trust to others. This does not mean that you must actually perform all of the administrative work yourself. You can delegate certain administrative details to persons qualified to handle them. For example, you can employ an agent to collect rents. However, the responsibility for the administration of the trust always remains with you as Trustee even if you delegate some duties to others.

If you are one of two or more co-Trustees, you cannot rely on the other co-Trustee(s) to administer the trust. You must participate in the administration. If another co-Trustee acts improperly with respect to trust matters, you have the obligation to correct the situation. You have an obligation to be aware of what other co-Trustees are doing on behalf of the trust. Each co-Trustee is responsible to the beneficiaries for the misconduct and breaches of duty of the other co-Trustee(s). Consider an important part of your job as being the watchman for the beneficiaries. If something goes wrong, do not let it go wrong on your watch. Report the actions to the beneficiaries and, if necessary, to the court with the appropriate jurisdiction.

Duty to account

Another of your basic duties, which will be discussed in further detail in the next chapters, is your duty to account to the beneficiaries. Beneficiaries are entitled to be kept reasonably informed about their interests in the trust. Note that different beneficiaries may have different interests in the trust, and you are duty bound to account to each beneficiary only with respect to that beneficiary's interest. Most trust instruments, and the California Statutes, require at least annual accounting to the beneficiaries.

Duty to segregate trust assets

You must keep the trust property separate and distinct from your own property. In other words, you should have a separate bank account or accounts for the trust, and you must not put either trust principal or income into your personal account(s). Trust assets must always be readily identifiable as such, and must be segregated from your other property.

Duty to get help if you need it

Should any questions arise as to the proper interpretation of the terms of the trust instrument, you should consult the attorney for the trust. If there is a question regarding taxes or financial investments, you should consult the appropriate tax professional or financial advisor. "Flying from the seat of your pants" is dangerous, because it can expose you to personal liability if something goes wrong. On the other hand, your reliance on the advice of a competent and qualified professional can be a defense to a claim that you breached a fiduciary duty.

Duty to protect and preserve trust assets

You have the duty to protect and preserve the trust assets, and to insure them whenever practicable. Be sure to consult a competent insurance professional regarding proper coverage for trust assets. Few things are worse than having a trust asset destroyed, through no fault of yours, and then discovering that the asset was not insured. In that case, your own personal bank account becomes the insurance company.

Avoiding the appearance of impropriety

You will find very little sympathy with a judge or jury if you do something that looks like it may be improper, whether or not it really is. If someone questions your activities as Trustee, you may find yourself having the burden of proving that you acted properly. You do not have the advantage of being presumed innocent until you are proven guilty. Most of the time, you will find the contrary presumption working against you. Wise Trustees do their best to be completely above reproach.

CHAPTER FOUR
THE CONDUCT OF THE TRUSTEE

The law does not demand absolute perfection from you. However, it does demand absolute **loyalty**, absolute **honesty**, and complete and accurate **disclosure**, even if that disclosure could cast you in an uncomfortably negative light. In the classic words of Judge Benjamin Cardozo (who went on to become a justice of the United States Supreme Court):

> Many forms of conduct permissible in a workaday world for those acting at arm's length are forbidden to those bound by fiduciary ties. A trustee is held to something stricter than the morals of the market place. Not honesty alone, but the punctilio of an honor the most sensitive, is then the standard of behavior. As to this there has developed a tradition that is unbending and inveterate. Uncompromising rigidity has been the attitude of courts of equity when petitioned to undermine the rule of undivided loyalty by the "disintegrating erosion" of particular exceptions. . . . Only thus has the level of conduct for fiduciaries been kept at a level higher than that trodden by the crowd. . . .

Meinhard v. Salmon, 249 N.Y. 458, 464, 164 N.E. 545, 546 (1928).

TITLE TO TRUST ASSETS

Whenever you take title to an asset as Trustee, you should pay close attention to how that title is vested or documented. The terms of the trust will identify its name. Generally, title should be vested in:

[Trustee's Name], Trustee, under the *[Trust Name]*, dated *[Trust Date]*.

Or

[Trustee 1's Name] and *[Trustee 2's Name]*, Trustees, under the *[Trust Name]*, dated *[Trust Date]*.

When you sign documents, including checks, you should sign your name as "*[Your Name]*, Trustee." By signing as "Trustee," you will not be held personally liable as long as the action you are taking is within the scope of your authority as Trustee. This rule does not apply to a Trustee who is also the trust creator- it only applies to successor Trustees.

HOW TO SIGN DOCUMENTS

California State Probate Statutes state that "[u]nless otherwise provided in the contract, a trustee is personally liable on contracts entered into in the trustee's fiduciary capacity in the course of the administration of the trust estate." In other words, unless you take pains to document that you are signing a contract as a Trustee and not as an individual, you will be inviting personal liability for whatever the contract requires. Accordingly, whenever you sign any document on behalf of the trust, always sign as *"[Your Name], Trustee."* It must be absolutely clear that you are obligating the trust and not yourself. If you do this (assuming you were acting within the scope of your authority as Trustee when you signed a document), you will not be personally liable for any obligation under that document.

SOURCES OF YOUR AUTHORITY AS TRUSTEE

Your authority comes first and foremost from the trust instrument, and your duties and powers as described there are your primary instructions. You should read the trust instrument with care, and from time to time read it again. The trust instrument may contain specific provisions that take precedence over the general rules that apply to trusts—even the ones mentioned in this manual. However, note that there are certain basic rules relating to trusts that will apply no matter what the trust instrument says. For example, a trust instrument cannot allow or encourage illegal activity against public policy on the part of the Trustee or the beneficiaries.

The second source of your authority comes from the California State Probate Statutes. Various provisions of the California Statutes cover things that are not specifically spelled out in the trust instrument. The Uniform Trustees Powers Act (California Probate Code Section 16200-16249), the Uniform Prudent Investor Act (California Probate Code Section 16040-16054), the Uniform Principal and Income Act (California Probate Code Section 16320-16375), and the California Probate Code hold particular relevance to your role as Trustee.

The third source of your authority is found in the court decisions relating to trusts. This is known as the "common law." The common law of California is found primarily in the opinions of our State's Supreme Court and our Intermediate Court of Appeals, but California courts may follow decisions from other jurisdictions as well as the Federal Ninth Circuit Court of Appeals and the United States Supreme Court.

You need to keep all three of these sources of authority in mind as you carry out your duties as Trustee. You also need to remember that other laws, such as the **Internal Revenue Code** and the Treasury Regulations and court decisions that interpret the Code, will dictate what you can or should do in many circumstances. This should convince you that you will need to rely on the advice and guidance of your legal counsel, your accountant, and your other trusted advisors throughout your tenure as Trustee.

CHAPTER FIVE
A LISTING OF THE SUCCESSOR TRUSTEE'S INITIAL RESPONSIBILITIES

When the successor Trustee takes over the role of Trustee, whether due to the death, incapacity, resignation or removal of the original or former Trustee, the initial work will include some or all of the following tasks. The particular tasks necessary for the successor Trustee to complete will depend on whether the Trustmaker is incapacitated or deceased.

If the Trustmaker is *incapacitated* or *deceased* and you are named as the Trustee or Executor, here is a listing of typical tasks to be accomplished within the few weeks after you accept the role of Trustee:

1. Report to the beneficiaries early and often!

2. Set a meeting with an attorney experienced with trust administration. This meeting should take place within 30 days of the date of death, or determination of incapacity.

3. Determine what the assets are and how they are titled.

4. Determine the liabilities of the estate- the debts and obligations owed.

5. If deceased, notify a funeral director and clergy, and make an appointment to discuss funeral arrangements. Note that the person listed first on an Advance Health Care Directive generally has authority to see to the disposition of remains. The disposition of remains can become a serious issue in dysfunctional families. Contact by phone and notify the immediate family, close friends, business colleagues and employer of the decedent.

6. Notify the Trustmaker's financial advisor. Decisions may need to be made regarding repositioning financial assets and tax planning.

7. Telephone the Trustmaker's employer and speak with the employee benefits office and provide the following information: name, Social Security number, date of death (or incapacity); the company can then begin to process benefits immediately.

8. If the Trustmaker is deceased, request at least 10 certified copies of the decedent's death certificate. This can usually be arranged by the funeral home.

9. Contact the Social Security Administration if the decedent was receiving social security benefits. Note that the last month's check issued by the Social Security Administration may be reclaimed by Social Security. This is typically done by automatic withdrawal from the account, so you want to (1) be sure there are adequate funds left in the appropriate account, and (2) leave the appropriate account open for a time period long enough to allow Social Security to retrieve its payment.

10. Secure valuables and important papers. Consider removing valuables from the home.

11. Change the house locks unless the home or business is occupied by the spouse, beneficiary, or other trusted individual.

12. Determine immediate cash needs and identify accounts where cash is immediately available; determine what expenses need to be paid promptly.

13. Request that the Postmaster forward mail if appropriate.

14. Be sure utilities are maintained (gas, electricity, telephone). Do not have these shut off.

15. Cancel charge accounts, credit cards, and newspaper, magazine subscriptions, internet, cable TV, etc. and ask for refunds, if applicable. Also inquire as to possible insurance benefits on these accounts.

16. Make certain that property and casualty insurance coverage continues on any real estate and automobiles. **Only** if asked by the insurer, advise that the property is currently **unoccupied** if that is the case. You will want to review the insurance policy on the home or other real property to confirm coverage if the real property is vacant or unoccupied and whether there are time periods after which coverage will lapse if left unoccupied.

17. Confirm whether there is a safe deposit box. If yes, take an inventory of contents with the beneficiaries or a bank officer present before removing contents.

18. As possible, locate passwords needed to access on-line records. Note that it may be possible to reset passwords under

certain cases if you have personal identification information for the Trustmaker including their social security number.

19. Gather personal records, including checkbooks, recent statements if there are hard copies of them, and a copy of last year's tax return.

20. Gather all life insurance and accidental death insurance policies; do not forget to check with credit card companies that might make life insurance benefits available to their cardholders.

21. If the Trustmaker was ever in the military service, notify the Veterans' Administration. You may be eligible for death or disability benefits.

22. Do not do anything that would be out of the ordinary. Do not sell the house or the car, do not accept retirement plan benefits, do not take other significant actions.

Please note that this list is not a comprehensive list, nor does it substitute for legal advice. Every situation is different and getting legal advice at least once before proceeding can be invaluable. In addition to the practical steps outlined above, there are legal notices and requirements that must be implemented upon the death or incapacity of an individual, even if there is a living trust.

CHAPTER SIX
NOTIFICATION BY TRUSTEE

The trust administration begins with a notification to all trust beneficiaries and heirs of the incapacitated or deceased Trustmakers, as required by California law. Pursuant to California Probate Code Section 16061.7, the notification must be sent within 60 days of the date the trust becomes irrevocable, either due to the incapacity or death of the Trustmaker. If a copy of the trust is not provided with the notification, then the notification must inform the recipient that a copy of the trust will be made available if so requested.

After receipt of the notification, the recipient has 120 days from the date of mailing of the notification and copy of the trust to file a contest or objection to the terms of the trust. If no contest is filed within that time period, then the notification recipient may forfeit their right to file a contest to the terms of the trust agreement. However, if no notification is mailed by the Trustee, then the time period in which a trust contest could be filed based on the statute of limitations is greatly increased, and could be up to four years in length. Accordingly, the mailing of a notification by the Trustee is essential to help to minimize potential disputes during the trust administration process.

CHAPTER SEVEN
GETTING ASSETS INTO THE TRUST

One of your basic duties as Trustee is to marshal, or take control of the assets of the trust. This typically is a straight-forward process, in which you submit a Certification of Trust to the various financial institutions at which trust assets are held, confirming your authority to act as Trustee over the accounts. Once submitted, the accounts will be transferred to you as Trustee. Additionally, this includes filing the necessary documents to transfer title to the real property to you as Trustee.

But what happens if the Trustmaker did not initially title an account to the trust? If you have also been named as the Executor to the Pour-Over Will of the decedent, you are charged with a duty to marshal all assets that remained titled to the decedent as an individual as of their death, including assets that may have not been initially titled to the trust. There are two options for transferring these assets to the trust, prior to filing for a formal probate.

SMALL ESTATE AFFIDAVIT

If the total value of the assets left outside the trust equal $150,000 or less, and those assets do not include real property, you do not have to go to court to have these assets transferred to the trust. Instead, these assets may be transferred by submission of a Small Estate Affidavit to each institution. The Small Estate Affidavit confirms your legal right to inherit the property as Trustee of the decedent's trust. Many banks and other institutions have their own Small Estate Affidavit form. However, if the institution does not have its own, an attorney can prepare a Small Estate Affidavit for your use.

HEGGSTAD PETITION

A California "Heggstad" Petition is a way to transfer assets to the trust when those assets do not qualify for a Small Estate Affidavit. If the total value of assets left outside the trust equal more than $150,000, or those assets include real property, a court order confirming the property as an asset of the trust will be required for you, as Trustee, to obtain title and control over those assets without a formal probate process. For a Heggstad Petition to be approved, you must show that the Trustmaker had the intent to have those asset in their trust when they died. Intent may be evidenced by the schedule of assets attached to the trust, or by a specific reference to the asset in the terms of the trust. An attorney should be contacted to guide you through this process and represent you in the court proceedings.

CHAPTER EIGHT
ACCOUNTING FOR ASSETS IN THE ESTATE, AND ACCOUNTING FOR MONEY IN AND OUT OF THE ESTATE

In our experience, this is the area that gets most Trustees in trouble. You must set up and keep an accurate set of books documenting the administration. You do not need to be an accountant to do this, but you might want to engage an accountant or, at the very least, a professional bookkeeper, to assist you. Your records should show all assets you receive, hold, and disburse, with the date, amount, and explanation of each. California Statutes require you to keep the beneficiaries reasonably informed about the trust and its administration, although no beneficiary of a revocable living trust, other than the Trustmaker, has the right to information about the trust during the Trustmaker's lifetime.

If the persons who receive trust income (also known as *current income beneficiaries*) are different from those who will receive the principal when the trust terminates (also known as *remaindermen*), your records should classify all receipts and disbursements as *income* or *principal*. In most cases, there will be no difficulty about this. Things like rent, ordinary dividends, and interest are clearly income; and generally, proceeds from the sale of an asset are principal.

Many trust instruments contain instructions to guide the Trustee in resolving these and other accounting problems, and you may find all of the guidance you need from this source. If you do not, you (with the assistance of your attorney and your accountant) will need to consult the Uniform Principal and Income Act of the California Probate Code.

If you keep your accounts carefully, it will be a simple matter for your accountant to find all of the information necessary to prepare trust tax returns, reports to the beneficiaries, or reports to the court, if that becomes necessary.

Remember that the trust you are administering is a separate "person" in the eyes of the law, and although it has no physical body, it may have its own tax identification number. A clear set of books creates a record of its healthy and independent life.

You are entitled to reimbursement of your reasonable expenses incurred in the administration of the trust. You are also entitled to a reasonable fee for services rendered, but you are not required to take a fee. If you do, it should be added to your other income and reported on your personal income tax return. You will also need to file California personal income tax returns and pay State taxes with respect to your Trustee compensation.

You should be prepared to render an accounting at least once a year. Any beneficiary may demand such an accounting, and even if none does, your annual accounting should be a permanent part of the records of your administration of the trust.

The trust beneficiaries are entitled to copies of the trust instrument (at least the portions of the trust instrument that relate to their specific beneficial interests and if requested within 120 days of the notification of trust), and they may also be entitled to examine the books and records of the trust. This is another good reason for you to maintain your books in a scrupulous manner.

Your annual accounting should include the following elements:

- An inventory of all trust assets, any changes in the status of the assets, and the approximate fair market value of each asset;

- Detailed information regarding all trust bank accounts, including bank statements;

- The nature of all investments, together with proper backup information;

- Any and all insurance, of all types, in force for the trust assets or for a beneficiary, and the dates and amounts of all premium payments;

- All debts of the trust and pertinent information about each debt, including the nature of the debt and the identity of the creditor;

- A list of all known claims presented to the Trustee and pertinent information about each claim, such as the identity of the claimant, the nature of the claim, and what action the Trustee took regarding that claim;

- All receipts that have come into the trust and how those receipts were derived;

- All disbursements made from the trust, to whom each disbursement was made, the purpose of the disbursement, and whether the disbursement came out of principal or income;

- A statement that all tax returns have been filed;

- A statement that all taxes and bond premiums (if any) have been paid; and

- A statement specifying the Trustee's compensation and how that compensation was calculated.

You would be wise to have the beneficiaries sign written receipts for all distributions, and to have them sign approvals of your annual accountings as they are provided. You will have the option of asking a court to review and approve your accountings if any of the beneficiaries do not approve them.

CHAPTER NINE
A TRUSTEE'S DUTY TO PRUDENTLY INVEST ESTATE ASSETS

You must keep the trust assets invested appropriately. It is important for you to remember that if you are serving as a Trustee for someone other than yourself, you will be held to a higher standard of care than you would be if you were simply investing your own funds.

A trust instrument may limit, permit deviations from, or elimate the following rules, and, to the extent the Trustee acts in reasonable reliance on the terms of the trust instrument, the Trustee cannot be faulted by the beneficiaries. However, where the trust instrument is silent, or where it specifically adopts the California Statutes, the following rules apply. California's Uniform Prudent Investor Act ("UPIA"), is part of the California Probate Code. A summary of your responsibilities under the UPIA follows.

The general standard of care (that is, the standard against which your acts as Trustee will be measured in determining whether you discharged your investment duties properly) is found at California Probate Code Section 16047:

Standard of care; portfolio strategy; risk and return objectives.

a) A Trustee shall invest and manage trust assets as a prudent investor would, by considering the purposes, terms, distribution requirements, and other circumstances of the trust. In satisfying this standard, the Trustee shall exercise reasonable care, skill, and caution.

b) A Trustee's investment and management decisions respecting individual assets and courses of action must be evaluated not in isolation, but in the context of the trust portfolio as a whole and as a part of an overall investment strategy having risk and return objectives reasonably suited to the trust.

c) Among circumstances that are appropriate to consider in investing and managing trust assets are the following, to the extent relevant to the trust or its beneficiaries:

(i)   General economic conditions.

(ii)   The possible effect of inflation or deflation.

(iii)   The expected tax consequences of investment decisions or strategies.

(iv)   The role that each investment or course of action plays within the overall trust portfolio.

(v)   The expected total return from income and the appreciation of capital.

(vi)   Other resources of the beneficiaries known to the Trustee as determined from information provided by the beneficiaries.

(vii) Needs for liquidity, regularity of income, and preservation or appreciation of capital.

(viii) An asset's special relationship or special value, if any, to the purposes of the trust or to one or more of the beneficiaries.

d) A Trustee shall make a reasonable effort to ascertain facts relevant to the investment and management of trust assets.

e) A Trustee may invest in any kind of property or type of investment or engage in any course of action or investment strategy consistent with the standards of this chapter.

You, as Trustee, have the duty to diversify the trust assets. This means that you should not place all of the trust's eggs in one basket. If all of the trust assets were invested in United Airlines stock, for example, and if there were a terrorist attack that resulted in huge losses for the airline industry, the value of the trust assets would take a tremendous hit. Thus, you need to diversify the trust assets and thereby minimize the risk that the trust could be impoverished by a downturn in any one stock or any one market segment. Bear in mind, however, that your duty to diversify is also driven by other circumstances. If, for example, you had the duty to pay a large trust obligation or to distribute trust assets to beneficiaries, it might be appropriate for all or a substantial portion of the trust assets to be in cash and not invested in other kinds of assets.

Within a "reasonable time" after accepting a Trusteeship or receiving trust assets, you are required to review the trust assets and make and implement decisions concerning the retention and disposition of assets, in order to bring the trust portfolio into compliance with the purposes, terms, distribution requirements, and other circumstances of the trust. What constitutes a "reasonable time" depends on the circumstances, but it certainly does not pay to dawdle. If the value of the trust assets declines significantly, and if you could have avoided the loss through diversification, you may very well have some unhappy beneficiaries on your hands.

You have the duty to be absolutely loyal to the trust and to be impartial toward the beneficiaries. Your duty of impartiality is driven by the kinds of interests held by the various beneficiaries. For example, some beneficiaries may have current rights to receive trust income, whereas others may have the right to receive trust property at some point in the future. You need to treat the beneficiaries in each class the same way, and you must not favor the current beneficiaries over the future beneficiaries unless the trust instrument allows you to do that.

Although the general rule is that Trustees cannot delegate any of their responsibilities to others, the UPIA acknowledges that delegating some of your responsibilities may very well be in the best interest of the trust. Thus, you are allowed to delegate investment functions and management functions to others, if that would be prudent in the circumstances. If, for example, you are not a Wall Street wiz, it is probably your duty to consult someone who is when you are developing the investment strategy for the trust. You can even delegate investment decision-making authority to expert asset managers if that would be appropriate, given the value and kind of trust assets for which you are responsible. Similarly, if the trust assets include real estate and you are not an ace real estate manager, there is nothing wrong with your engaging someone who is. You nevertheless have the duty to monitor the experts to whom you delegate responsibilities, and to make sure that they are faithfully serving the best interests of the trust.

The above summary is fairly comprehensive, but it is not exhaustive. Always remember that if ever you have questions about trust administration, you can and should call on the expertise of your legal counsel and other advisors.

CHAPTER TEN
REAL PROPERTY

Generally speaking, the Trustee has the authority to determine whether real property should be held by the trust and distributed in-kind to the beneficiaries, or sold by the trust prior to distribution to the beneficiaries. However, thanks to Propositions 13, 58, 60 and 90, there are now are special considerations to be made for real property in the State of California.

PROPOSITION 13 – REAL PROPERTY TAXES

In 1978, the voters in California passed Proposition 13 to reduce the property tax rates on homes, businesses and farms. Prior to the passage of Proposition 13, there were no limits on property tax rate increases. Ultimately, this caused many people to be unable to afford to stay in their family homes or businesses.

Under Proposition 13, property tax values were frozen at their 1976 assessed values, and tax rate increases were limited to no more than 2% per year or Consumer Price Index ("CPI"), whichever is the lesser of the two, so long as the property was held and not sold. Upon sale, the property tax basis (assessed value) was to be reassessed at 1% of the sale price, and the yearly cap of the 2% increase in property tax would be again applicable going forward.

Finally, with Proposition 13 homeowners were able to estimate what their future property taxes would be, thus allowing them to plan appropriately and ultimately have confidence that they would be able to financially stay in their homes or businesses.

PROPOSITION 58 – CLAIM FOR REASSESSMENT EXCLUSION

Proposition 58 became effective on November 6, 1986, and covers transfers of title in California real property from parent(s) to child(ren) or from child(ren) to parent(s). Generally speaking, under Proposition 58 any real estate that is transferred from parent(s) to child(ren), or from child(ren) to parent(s), may be excluded from reassessment for property tax purposes. These transfers can include transfers by deed, inheritance, or court order.

Specifically, this proposition allows for the transfer of the primary residence regardless of its value, and $1,000,000 of the "assessed roll value" (**not** market value) on transfers of non-primary residence property, such as rental properties or vacation properties. The $1 million limit on transfers of non-primary residence properties is a per person limit. Thus, if properly planned for, a married couple may transfer to their children both their primary residence and $2,000,000 of "assessed roll value" on non-primary residence properties in California.

Transfers between legal entities such as corporations, partnerships, or limited liability companies that are owned by parents or children do not qualify for the Proposition 58 exclusion. There may be special circumstances in which a grandparent(s) to grandchild(ren) transfer may qualify for the Proposition 58 exclusion, however certain additional requirements must be met for this to be applicable.

In order to qualify any transfers under Proposition 58 as excludable from reassessment for property tax purposes, a Claim for Reassessment Exclusion for Parent to Child Transfer must be filed with the County Assessor's Office in the county where the real property is located.

Considerations for the Trustee and Beneficiaries

Because Proposition 58 allows for the transfer of real property to children without reassessment of property taxes, there are now significant advantages to maintaining real property that is inherited through a trust, will, or intestate succession.

If there is only one child inheriting through the trust, the decision may be an easy one. The child will be able to inherit the property with their parent's property tax basis, which will allow them to maintain the family home at a more reasonable expense. This is especially advantageous in areas where property values are extremely high. Additionally, if the child wishes to keep and rent the property as an investment property, the low carrying costs combined with the stepped-up income tax basis to the parent's date of death value will provide the child with significant income tax savings.

However, if there are multiple children inheriting through the trust, the decision may be more involved for the Trustee in ultimately determining whether to sell the property or distribute the property to the children. Considerations here will include:

- How well do the children get along?

- Will any of the children reside in the property? If so, will they be required to pay rent?

- If maintained as an investment property, will the children be able to manage going into business together?

- If one child wants the property as their distribution, are there sufficient funds to equalize the distribution to the other children?

These considerations are especially important prior to distribution of the property to the beneficiaries. If the property is distributed, and ownership is titled to more than one child, then there is no going back later on. If the children later decide that one child wants to hold the property and the others do not, any transfer at that point will be a transfer between siblings and will be subject to reassessment for property tax purposes on the portion transferred.

PROPOSITIONS 60 AND 90 – TRANSFER OF REAL PROPERTY TAXES

Propositions 60 and 90 allow for the transfer of base year value for property taxes under certain circumstances. Proposition 60 allows for the transfer within the same county (intra-county), and Proposition 90 allows for the transfer from one county to another county (intercounty). As of June 5, 2015, there were eleven counties in the State of California that have enacted an ordinance enabling the intercounty base year value transfer, including: Alameda, El Dorado, Los Angeles, Orange, Riverside, San Bernardino, San Diego, San Mateo, Santa Clara, Tuolumne, and Ventura.

There are strict eligibility requirements that must be met in order to qualify for a Proposition 60/90 transfer. These requirements include:

- The homeowner, or spouse residing with the homeowner, must have been at least 55 years of age when the original property was sold;

- The original property must have been eligible for the homeowners' or disabled veterans' exemption, either at the time of sale or within two (2) years of the purchase of the replacement property;

- The replacement property must be the homeowner's principal residence and eligible for the homeowners' exemption or disabled veterans' exemption;

- The replacement property must be of equal or lesser fair market value than the original property. This test applies to the entire replacement property, even if the homeowner only purchases a partial interest in the replacement property; and

- The replacement property must be purchased, or built, within two (2) years of the sale of the original property. This time requirement may be two (2) years before or after.

In order to qualify a transfer under Proposition 60 or Proposition 90, a Claim of Person(s) at Least 55 Years of Age for Transfer of Base Year Value to Replacement Dwelling form must be filed with the County Assessor's Office. Additionally, it is important to note that a senior citizen may transfer his or her base year value under Propositions 60 and 90 **only once**.

Considerations for the Trustee and Beneficiaries

The benefit of Propositions 60 and 90 may be a significant consideration for senior beneficiaries. When used together with the Proposition 58 benefits, a senior beneficiary may be able to inherit their parent's low property tax basis and then transfer that basis either to a new property in the same county, or a new property in another county that allows for an intercounty base value transfer. Accordingly, if a senior beneficiary is considering moving within 2 years of the distribution of trust assets, it would be prudent to discuss with them the benefits of establishing primary residence status in any real property owned by the trust in order to be eligible under Proposition 60/90.

CHAPTER ELEVEN
INCOME TAXES AND ESTATE TAXES

The Internal Revenue Code considers a revocable living trust to be a "grantor trust" during the lifetime of its maker. As a general rule, such a trust is not required to file income tax returns. Treas. Reg. §1.671-4(b). Moreover, the Trustmaker's Social Security Number is the initial taxpayer identification number for the trust—at least for as long as the Trustmaker is alive. The Trustees of all other types of trusts may be required to obtain taxpayer identification numbers (by filing a Form SS-4 with the IRS) and file fiduciary income tax returns (Form 1041) with the IRS and analogous forms with the states in which the trusts derive income. The obligation to file a Form 1041 arises if the trust had any "taxable income" or had "gross income" of $600.00 or more, regardless of the amount of "taxable income" in any taxable year.

You are well advised, particularly if you are a layman, to seek professional assistance in the preparation of tax returns, since they do differ substantially from personal income tax returns. We recommend that you consult, if not retain, a qualified income tax professional, a Certified Public Accountant (CPA), Public Account (PA) or an Enrolled Agent (EA).

If the estate is over the amount that can pass to the beneficiaries without incurring an estate tax, the Federal Estate Tax Return or an extension must be filed within 9 months of the date of death. The tax is due at the nine month mark, even if the extension is filed. The extension provides for a 6 month period at the end of which time the federal estate tax return must be filed. The good news is that California no longer has an inheritance tax or estate tax so only a timely filed federal estate tax return is required.

If the beneficiary of the estate includes a surviving spouse, then even though an estate tax may not be due, consideration must be given to the filing of an estate tax return to preserve the deceased spouse's federal estate tax exemption amount under the "portability" rules established by Congress in 2013.

While the preparation and filing of a federal estate tax return is a relatively complex and time consuming event, a surviving spouse will want to explore with counsel and the tax profes-sional retained as to the advisability of filing the federal estate tax return to preserve the deceased spouse's unused exemption amount. This is a "use it or lose it" proposition and if a timely estate tax return is not filed, the opportunity to pass an estate tax savings to the ultimate beneficiaries of a married couple's estate will be lost.

CHAPTER TWELVE
COMPENSATION FOR TRUSTEES

Trustees are entitled to compensation for their services, which compensation is governed by instructions in the trust instrument. If the trust instrument is silent on the issue of Trustee compensation, Probate Code Section 15681 provides that the Trustee is entitled to "reasonable compensation." What constitutes reasonable compensation is subject to interpretation, and it is therefore recommended that the Trustee take only that compensation which is generally considered as acceptable by the court in the county in which the trust is being administered.

Typically, a court will not be involved in a trust administration, and will therefore not determine what is considered reasonable compensation. However, in cases where court intervention has been necessary in determining reasonable compensation, the courts have looked to factors including:

- The gross income of the trust estate;

- The success or failure of the Trustee's administration;

- The time spent in the performance of the Trustee's duties;

- The fidelity or disloyalty of the Trustee in putting the best interests of the beneficiaries ahead of his or her own best interests;

- Risk and responsibility assumed by the Trustee, such as a Trustee taking on the responsibility of running a business owned by the trust during the administration process;

- The qualifications of the Trustee and any unusual skill, expertise or experience of the Trustee, such as the Trustee being an accountant, attorney, real estate agent, or holding some other professional license or qualification that may enable savings during the administration; and

- The custom in the community.

Though you are entitled to reasonable compensation and reimbursement of your reasonable expenses incurred in the administration of the trust, you are not required to take compensation. If you do take compensation for your services, you need to be aware that Trustee fees are taxable as ordinary income to the Trustee. Accordingly, any compensation received by the Trustee should be reported on the Trustee's personal income tax return. However, inheritance that the Trustee may receive as a beneficiary of the trust instrument is generally income-tax free. In waiving compensation for the Trustee, you may ultimately keep more resources in the trust and avoid paying unnecessary taxes.

Though the trust may not require approval of fees by the beneficiaries, you may wish to present both your timesheets and expense sheets to the beneficiaries, with a copy of the accounting, for each beneficiary's review and approval prior to paying yourself fees or reimbursement out of the trust. This will help to prevent any disputes regarding the work performed and the amount of fees taken by the Trustee, which can ultimately be a contestable issue in court.

CHAPTER THIRTEEN
AT THE END, THE TRUSTEE WILL UNDERTAKE THE DISTRIBUTIONS OF THE ESTATE

Let us turn now to the thing that is of primary interest to the beneficiaries: when and under what circumstances they receive distributions.

The trust instrument should tell you who is to receive benefits from the trust and when those benefits are to be paid. It may also give you certain discretionary powers with regard to distributions.

Some of the problems that can arise in exercising your discretionary powers are illustrated by the following example.

The trust instrument gives you the power, in your sole discretion, to distribute income or principal or both among your sister's three children to provide for their maintenance, support, and education. Sarah has graduated from college and is doing very well. Beth is "doing her thing" in San Francisco, while Drew is doing average work as a freshman in college and is something of a sports car nut. You receive a request from: Sarah for $35,000 for her graduate school tuition for the coming year (to be spent at a university in Europe), Beth for $10,000 for medical expenses as she is undernourished and high on drugs, and Drew for $40,000 for a car. Which of these requests can you honor under the standards given?

For Sarah: Education is a proper purpose of the trust, but does it have to be in Europe? Perhaps Sarah will get just as good of an education in the United States for half the cost. If you enable Sarah to go to Europe, Beth and Drew could later claim that you abused your discretion or even breached your fiduciary duty to the trust to the extent that $35,000 exceeds the cost of Sarah's education at a comparable stateside institution. If you do decide to allow Sarah to go to Europe for her education, you should make certain to document some very good reasons for her going there instead of staying in the United States.

For Beth: Support and maintenance are proper purposes, but do these terms include medical expenses or are they intended to be limited to ordinary living expenses such as room and board? The trust instrument may or may not tell you. You may also be stuck in the quandary of trying to decide whether spending money for Beth's medical care, without also requiring her to undergo some kind of drug treatment, is prudent.

For Drew: Does support and maintenance include a car if Drew has access to a reliable car now? What if Drew has a part-time job and needs transportation?

In all three cases, the trust instrument may provide you adequate guidance. However, if it does not you have your work cut out for you. Your primary objective should be to carry out the intent of the person who created the trust, if that can be determined from the trust instrument. You should also consider the size of the trust, the amount of income the trust generates, the needs and convenience of the beneficiaries, and the various other demands that the trust might be called upon to meet.

Remember that when your permissible sphere of action is limited by a standard, you must observe that standard or risk a lawsuit for breach of trust or breach of a fiduciary duty. You are personally liable (meaning that your own assets are at risk) if you lose a lawsuit in which you are accused of violating your fiduciary duties.

Also remember that if you are presented with an issue that cannot easily be resolved, you always have the option of petitioning a court for instructions. If you pass up the opportunity to petition the court and end up making a wrong decision, you can be sure that if a beneficiary sues you, the court will not regard you with great favor.

This short manual cannot outline all of the problems you may face in connection with the exercise of your discretionary powers, but the above example should encourage you to analyze every distribution for possible problems before taking action. There is never any harm in consulting your legal counsel and other advisors if issues come up, and doing so can help you stay out of hot water.

If you are administering a trust at the time it terminates, you should provide the beneficiaries a final accounting. Your final accounting should include the following:

- The property, rents, revenues, and profits received since your last accounting that was approved by all of the beneficiaries or by the court;

- The disposition of the property, rents, revenues, and profits;

- The debts and expenses of the trust that remain unpaid;

- The property that remains in the hands of the Trustee;

- A statement that the Trustee has paid all required bond premiums, insurance premiums, and any other payments that the Trustee is required to keep current;

- A description of the tax returns filed by the Trustee during the term of the trust;

- A complete accounting of the taxes that the Trustee paid during the term of the trust;

- A description of all current delinquencies in the filing of tax returns or the payment of taxes, and the reasons for each delinquency; and

- Other facts that should be disclosed to convey a full, complete, and definite understanding of the condition of the trust.

You should ask the beneficiaries to sign a document in which they approve your accounting, waive any claims against you, and promise to pay any trust expenses that arise after they have received the trust assets. Remember that the beneficiaries' promise to pay those obligations is only as good as their ability to hold on to the assets you distribute to them, and it would behoove you to be very sure that all trust obligations have been paid before you make final distributions.

If any of the beneficiaries decline to approve your final account, you can petition a court to review and approve your account and discharge you from all further liability.

CHAPTER FOURTEEN
AVOIDING POTENTIAL LIABILITY

Three things can help you avoid personal liability in connection with serving as Trustee. First and foremost, *report early and often to the beneficiaries*. Keep the beneficiaries informed of your activities and the progress of the estate administration. Second, document all transactions, including any reasons for making or not making distributions. Third, think in terms of how your actions (or moments of inaction) could give rise to a lawsuit against you. While you may perceive the risk of getting sued as low in your case, you cannot ignore the possibility. When you are acting as a Trustee and are essentially in control of someone else's inheritance, you are not in the ideal situation since you can easily become the focus of any anger or frustration that beneficiaries may feel.

The best way to avoid lawsuits is to keep beneficiaries well informed of trust business and to be friendly and cooperative. Nobody really wants to sue someone who is considerate and communicates well, no matter how much that person may mess up. It is much more difficult to sue someone with whom you have a good relationship. On the other hand, someone who is difficult to get along with, who does not provide adequate information, and who communicates poorly is easy to sue because there is no valued relationship at stake.

If you are sued, having a carefully documented file is going to look far better to a judge and jury than having a file that is in disarray. Similarly, a Trustee who seeks advice from experts is going to look better than one who "wings it." In other words, from day one you must prepare for a lawsuit. It has been said that if one wants peace, one should prepare for war. A Trustee who is fully prepared for war, but not deliberately doing anything to start a war, is far more likely to avoid becoming a casualty of war.

Consider the dynamics of a lawsuit against a Trustee. Judges and juries alike tend to have more sympathy for the party that appears to be "right." If you have sloppy records (or have none), or if you have not sought help when you came up against something beyond your expertise, or if you have not provided beneficiaries with information that you should have, you will not be given the benefit of any doubt.

It may be tempting to take a shortcut to fix a problem or correct a poorly worded document. However, that is not your job. Only a court of proper jurisdiction can change a trust document, and even a court's authority to do that is limited. Do not take it upon yourself to deviate from what is written. The trust instrument is the best expression of the Trustmaker's intent. That expressed intent may be your best defense. You may not add to or subtract from the words of the document. You cannot be selective in carrying out various parts of the document. Consult your legal counsel if there is ever any question as to the correct interpretation of the trust instrument.

Your second line of defense is your ability to show how you carried out the intent of the trust. The better you do that, the more difficult it will be for a beneficiary (or anyone else) to show that you did something wrong.

Remember that once you accept the job of Trustee, you cannot get out of a lawsuit merely by resigning. Also bear in mind that the most common reason Trustees find themselves in trouble is because of actual or perceived self-dealing. Even if a trust instrument authorizes self-dealing, that does not make self-dealing a good idea. You should do your best to err on the side of avoiding self-dealing, or if it is appropriate in your mind get court approval.

If you ever wish to stop serving as Trustee, you can resign. However, your job (and the attendant duties and potential liability) does not end until a replacement Trustee steps into your shoes and all of the trust assets are transferred to your replacement.

It is common for the lawyer who drafted the trust instrument to represent successor Trustees, but there is no rule that says the successor Trustees are stuck with the attorney who prepared the trust. You have a duty to seek competent legal counsel, and you will need to assess whether that is a role that the drafting attorney can fill. Even if the drafting attorney is competent and highly regarded, you may not feel at ease communicating with him or her. When you choose your legal counsel, you should give some consideration to how comfortable you feel with that person. Your attorney should inspire trust and confidence, and should be someone with whom you can be completely frank and honest.

CHAPTER FIFTEEN
SURVIVING SPOUSE AS SOLE TRUSTEE

In a shared revocable living trust, or a family revocable living trust, both spouses are typically the initial Trustmakers and the initial Trustees. Typically, when the first spouse dies the surviving spouse will continue to serve alone in the role of Trustee. However, depending on family circumstances, a co-Trustee may be designated to serve with the surviving spouse as co-Trustees. Regardless as to whether you, as surviving spouse, serve independently or with another, there are certain administration tasks to be considered by the surviving spouse that are distinct, and that are in addition to those tasks designated to successor Trustees as discussed in the next chapters.

ESTATE TAX PLANNING

A family living trust may employ the use of sub-trusts at the death of the first spouse, in order to provide planning for various circumstances including estate tax savings, protection for blended families, and protection from creditors and predators. These sub-trusts have many different names, and are often times referred to as A/B Trusts, or A/B/C Trusts.

While the inheritance tax in California was repealed long ago, California residents do still need to be aware of and plan for the Federal Estate Tax. The first Federal Estate Tax was enacted in 1916, and from 1916 to 2017 there have been approximately 30 different exemption limits to the Federal Estate Tax. An exemption limit to the Federal Estate Tax means that an estate with a total value of assets that is equal to, or less than, the exemption amount will not be subject to federal estate taxation. However, if an estate has a total value of assets that is more than the exemption amount, anything over the exemption amount will be subject to federal estate taxation.

With what seems to be an ever-changing Federal Estate Tax exemption, trusts that called for the creation of an estate tax savings trust (often referred to as a "B Trust", "Bypass Trust", or "Exemption Trust") in order to plan for an estate tax exemption in 2004 at $1,500,000, may no longer be necessary when the first spouse dies in 2017 with a federal estate tax exemption of $5,490,000.

If in fact the original tax planning called for in the trust is no longer necessary, you may consider modification of the trust by court order to remove the now unnecessary tax planning language. As with any trust modification, there are both advantages and disadvantages to removing these provisions.

ADVANTAGES AND DISADVANTAGES TO NOT HAVING THE TAX PLANNING SUB-TRUST

A Bypass Trust is an irrevocable trust that is designed as an estate tax planning sub-trust to be created and funded upon the death of the first spouse. By eliminating the Bypass Trust provisions, you eliminate the additional administration tasks that will be required with an irrevocable sub-trust in place. When an irrevocable sub-trust is created, the assets titled to the sub-trust must be administered separately from all other assets. Unlike a revocable trust, an irrevocable trust is treated as a separate legal entity that is independent from the creator of the trust for tax purposes. Accordingly, Bypass Trust income is reportable under a separate tax identification number for the Bypass Trust, and the Trustee must file a tax return for the Bypass Trust even though the income generated by the trust is typically transferred to the surviving spouse's income tax return and taxed there.

Disadvantages to removing tax planning language

As noted above, the Bypass Trust is irrevocable and therefore at least partially protected from creditors and predators because it is a legal entity separate and apart from yourself as the surviving spouse. The surviving spouse does not personally own the assets in an irrevocable trust. Rather you own the assets as Trustee, not as an individual. Additionally, the surviving spouse will typically have limited use of the principal of the assets in the Bypass Trust, and will not be permitted to change the terms or the beneficiaries of the Bypass Trust. Accordingly, the assets in the irrevocable trust are considered to be separate and apart from your estate and cannot therefore be taken away from you without the creditor overcoming some significant hurdles. There is no creditor protection for assets held in the Survivor's Trust, as those assets are deemed to be owned by the surviving spouse individually.

Furthermore, because the value of assets placed in the Bypass Trust is generally limited to the value of the estate tax exemption available to the deceased spouse's estate (the value of exemption as of the date of death of the deceased spouse), there is no estate tax payable on those assets at the death of the first spouse. Moreover, as an estate tax savings trust, the value of the assets in the Bypass Trust are essentially "frozen" as of the date of death of the first spouse. Increases in value of Bypass Trust assets are therefore not considered in determining the estate tax due at the death of the surviving spouse.

The assets in the revocable Survivor's Trust will be exempt from taxation if the total value of those assets is less than the estate tax exemption at the time of the surviving spouse's death. In other words, without the use of Bypass Trust you are giving up the "estate tax freeze" on a portion of the trust assets if the Bypass Trust is not funded. If in future years, while you are still alive, the Federal Government were to reduce the estate tax exemption to an amount below the value of the estate at the time of your death, the estate would be exposed to the Federal Estate Tax. To ameliorate this outcome, you may wish to consult with a tax professional to file an estate tax return for your deceased spouse's estate claiming "portability" of their unused estate tax exemption without creating an irrevocable trust. However, if this return is not timely filed within 9 months of the first spouse's death, the surviving spouse will no longer be able to claim portability and this amelioration tactic will not be available to the estate.

Ultimately, the purpose for including tax planning language has changed dramatically in recent years. What planning was necessary for an estate tax exemption of $600,000 in 1996, may simply no longer apply to an estate tax exemption of $5,490,000 in 2017. Accordingly, the advantages to removing the tax planning language, as discussed below, may now outweigh the disadvantages for some estate plans.

Advantages to removing tax planning language

The discussion above regarding the provisions for the Bypass Trust is in stark contrast to the Survivor's Trust, a revocable sub-trust in which all assets continue to be in the complete control of the surviving spouse and are administered under the surviving spouse's social security number.

The surviving spouse is completely free to use the assets in the Survivor's Trust for whatever purpose you deem fit. However, the terms of the Bypass Trust are more restrictive with regard to what the surviving spouse can do with the assets. The Bypass Trust will generally require that the income generated by assets in the trust be paid to the surviving spouse. However, there is typically a restriction on the surviving spouse's use of the principal of the trust, which can include principal only being used for your health, education, maintenance or support.

For the beneficiaries, there is another advantage in keeping the property in the Survivor's Trust rather than requiring a mandatory division between the Survivor's Trust and the Bypass Trust. In the event that assets are held in a revocable trust until the surviving spouse's death, the beneficiaries will receive an adjustment to the income tax basis, also referred to as a "step-up" in the income tax basis if the asset has appreciated since the time of purchase, on the entire asset equal to its value on the date of the surviving spouse's death. This step-up in basis will allow the beneficiaries to avoid a capital gains tax if the Trustee's decision is to sell trust assets shortly upon the surviving spouse's death. If the assets are divided between revocable and irrevocable sub-trusts, the portion of those assets allocated to the irrevocable Bypass Trust will retain the tax basis it received at the time of the first spouse's death. In other words, the assets in the irrevocable Bypass Trust will receive an adjusted basis on the first spouse's death, but will not receive a second adjusted basis upon the second spouse's death. Again, if we assume real property values and investment assets will continue to increase over time, there will be built-in capital gain which will be "trapped" in the Bypass Trust and, unless the property is the subject of an exchange, an income tax will have to be paid on the gain.

At the death of the surviving spouse, if the assets were divided between the sub-trusts, those assets held in the Bypass Trust would be distributed pursuant to the directions established by both spouses at the time of the creation of the trust. Because the terms of the Bypass Trust make it irrevocable at the death of the first spouse, the surviving spouse is not permitted to change the beneficiaries on that trust.

However, if the trust assets are distributed to the Survivor's Trust, the ultimate distribution of the property remains under the surviving spouse's complete control. Elimination of the Bypass Trust means you are then free to change this distribution plan at any time, and a change in the distribution plan would affect 100% of the trust assets, not 50% of the trust assets. While this allows great flexibility to the surviving spouse, from the stand-point of the beneficiaries this flexibility could conceivably result in their disinheritance.

MODIFICATION BY COURT ORDER

If you, as the surviving spouse, make the determination that the tax planning sub-trust is no longer necessary for the estate, then modification of the trust to eliminate this language may be done through a petition for a court order modifying the trust. The petition may be based on two legal arguments under the California Probate Code, the first being a change in circumstances and the second being agreement between the beneficiaries. With this petition, notice will need to be given to all interested parties, including the remainder beneficiaries of the estate or those who will inherit any remaining trust assets upon your death. If the remainder beneficiaries object, the court may not grant the modification. Accordingly, it is recommended that you consult with an attorney prior to proceeding with the modification of a trust.

BLENDED FAMILIES

A blended family is a family in which at least one spouse has a child from a prior relationship or marriage. Now quite common, blended families come in all different shapes and sizes, and the dynamics of how the estate plan will be affected will differ greatly based on the type of family situation. For instance, a family where the husband and wife remarry young and with minor children will likely have a more simplified family estate plan treating all children as equal. Whereas a family where the husband and wife remarry at an older age, and with older children, may in fact have a more complex and sophisticated style of estate plan to accommodate the interfamilial relationships involved.

How the estate plan is established will affect how the surviving spouse will be able to manage the assets after the death of the first spouse. For most estate plans for married couples, the goal is to provide for the surviving spouse upon the death of the first spouse. However, in blended families there may be concerns about remarriage by the surviving spouse, or potential future disinheritance of the deceased spouse's child(ren). In a simple estate plan, where all assets pass to the surviving spouse in a Survivor's Trust and are therefore subject to total control by the surviving spouse, there will be no guarantee that the deceased spouse's children will benefit from the estate after the surviving spouse's death.

With a Survivor's Trust only, the surviving spouse can make gifts during their lifetime, or can change the distribution plan for all assets to his or her children, or even to a new spouse. This can ultimately lead to leaving little to no assets to pass to the deceased spouse's children. If this is a concern, then during the estate planning process the Trustmakers may implement a more complex plan including irrevocable sub-trusts to protect the future deceased spouse's share of the trust assets.

In a tax savings plan, there may be one or two irrevocable sub-trusts created upon the death of the first spouse, to hold the deceased spouse's assets during the surviving spouse's remaining lifetime. This is often referred to in a simplified manner as A/B trust planning, or A/B/C trust planning, in which the "B" and "C" trusts are irrevocable sub-trusts designated to hold the deceased spouse's half of the community property in the trust, and any of the deceased spouse's separate property. Being irrevocable, the assets allocated to these trusts are held pursuant to the terms of the original trust agreement, where the terms directing the management and distribution of the B and C Trusts can no longer be changed, modified or revoked after one spouse passes. Though these assets are protected for the future benefit of the Trustmakers' children, the surviving spouse still has the benefit of the assets during his or her lifetime. The surviving spouse typically will have the automatic right to all income generated by the assets allocated to the B and C Trusts. Additionally, there may be instructions included that allow the surviving spouse to access the principal of the B and C Trusts for certain identified purposes, such as for the health, education, maintenance or support of the surviving spouse.

For a surviving spouse who is a Trustee of a complex, blended family estate plan, it is important to know the best way to fulfill your fiduciary obligations to yourself as the primary beneficiary, and to all children as remainder beneficiaries of the trust. Though you may have no duty to presently account to all children as to your management of the trust assets during your lifetime, a lack of communication and transparency may create conflict between the children. After your death, any conflict previously created may lead to disputes between the children regarding their ultimate inheritance, which may conclude with all children in court disputing each other's claims. To prevent this, you should consult with an experienced estate planning attorney.

Updating the estate plan

Following the death of the first spouse, there may be reasons for the surviving spouse to modify the terms of the living trust and ancillary estate planning documents. If the deceased spouse is the only person named on the surviving spouse's Advance Health Care Directive, HIPAA Authorization, or Power of Attorney for Finances, it is most important to have these documents updated to name new agents to step into these roles if you become unwell or incapacitated.

As discussed above, your ability to modify the terms of the living trust as the surviving spouse depends on whether or not the original trust called for the creation of sub-trusts upon the death of the first spouse and whether those sub-trusts were in fact created and funded with assets. If all assets passed to you as the surviving spouse, without the creation of the sub-trusts, then you have complete control over the trust and may make whatever modifications you desire. This may include completely changing the distribution plan and the beneficiaries named to inherit the remaining assets upon your death. However, if sub-trusts were created and funded with a portion of the estate assets, you will only have the ability to change the terms of your portion of the assets in the Survivor's Trust or A Trust. In order to change the terms of the deceased spouse's portion of the assets, you will need to have the modification approved by a court order to be valid and effective upon your death.

CHAPTER SIXTEEN
RESIGNATION BY TRUSTEE

At any point in time, the current acting Trustee may no longer wish to serve in the role of Trustee and carry out the duties of the Trustee. Whether this is due to personal circumstances, lack of ability or incapacity, the trust agreement allows for the acting Trustee to resign from the role. To do so, the Trustee must follow the terms of the trust instrument with regard to providing notice of the resignation to certain parties to the trust instrument. If the trust instrument is silent on this issue, the acting Trustee may then resign by either petitioning the court, obtaining consent of the Trustmaker, or by obtaining the consent of all the beneficiaries of the trust instrument.

It is important to remember that, even though you have resigned as acting Trustee, your job (and the attendant duties and potential liability) does not end until a replacement Trustee takes over and all of the trust assets are transferred to them. An acting Trustee who abandons the role, without complying with the resignation requirements and ensuring the appointment of a successor Trustee, will remain liable for any mismanagement or neglect of trust property until that acting Trustee is formally removed and a new Trustee is appointed.

Upon resignation of an acting Trustee, a successor Trustee must be appointed. The trust instrument will generally either name a successor Trustee, an order for successor Trustees, or will provide instructions for the appointment of a successor Trustee if no others are named.

CHAPTER SEVENTEEN
CHECKLIST FOR GATHERING INFORMATION AS A PART OF THE ADMINISTRATION OF THE TRUST ESTATE

The following three chapters consist of checklists of tasks, some or all of which need to be accomplished by you as successor Trustee. Please remember that it is especially important for you to establish good accounting records promptly. These records will be needed for income tax purposes **and** for accounting to the beneficiaries of the trust. Additionally, it is essential that you report to the beneficiaries **early** and **often**. Open and clear communication with the beneficiaries is essential to your role as successor Trustee.

GATHERING OF INFORMATION

_____ 1. Prepare inventory of assets. An initial step in the administration process is to inventory and value the trust assets. It is important to value assets as of the **date of death** (or incapacity) because these values establish the worth of the Estate. As time goes on, you will account for income coming into the Estate and expenses going out of the Estate. You will liquidate assets in the Estate **at a gain or a loss based on the difference in value** of the assets between the date of death and the date of sale. Thus, establishing the date of death value on all assets is important. The only exception to this rule would be for any assets already in an irrevocable trust. These are typically seen in cases where one spouse has already passed away and the estate was divided into a Survivor's Trust and Bypass Trust.

_____ 2. Order an appraisal of real estate. This will typically be an appraisal of the primary residence. Again, the value established will be the date of death value. You will want to consider the use of a qualified appraiser rather than a realtor for this appraisal, as the valuation may later be subject to IRS scrutiny and a qualified appraiser's appraisal will typically hold up better in an audit than a realtor's market analysis.

_____ 3. Appraise valuable items or collections of personal property. This can be done by local jewelers, auction houses and, depending upon the expected value of the asset, consider an individual experienced in conducting Estate Sales.

_____ 4. Determine value of bank accounts at date of death (or incapacity). It is best to obtain the date of death valuations in writing from the bank. Otherwise values can usually be established through the bank statements for the month in which the death occurred.

_____ 5. Determine value of securities at date of death (or incapacity), including accrued interest or dividends. Because these accounts usually hold securities, which will receive an adjusted tax basis to the value of the security on the date of death, it is important to obtain the date of death valuations in writing from the brokerage house. Some brokerage houses charge a small fee for this service. It is well worth the fee to have the updated statement, which will be needed for the accounting and for tax returns.

_____ 6. Prepare spreadsheets for the trust accounting. It is critical that you, as a *fiduciary*, establish an accounting process early on and that you keep it updated. Most Trustee problems occur in this area. Do not delay in setting up and implementing your accounting system. Whatever your system, whether it be manual, though Quicken, or some other accounting method, remember that in most cases you may be required to provide the accounting to the beneficiaries. It needs to be comprehensive (that is, account for every penny) and it needs to be in a form that is understandable.

_____ 7. Keep the accounting updated and provide accountings to your attorney and your accountant as requested. In this vein, be sure your accountant knows you are keeping an accounting. The accounting information will be useful to your accountant in preparing income tax returns for the trust estate.

_____ 8. Prepare and mail a Notification by Trustee pursuant to Probate Code §16061.7 to all heirs and beneficiaries of the trust. This is required under California law. Preparation and service of the Notification must be done pursuant to the statute. Compliance is important as the Notification starts a 120-day period during which the *terms of the trust* may be challenged by any one of the individuals served.

_____ 9. Write to the beneficiaries of the trust outlining status and the further handling of the post mortem administration. This is not a statutory requirement. This is typically done by the attorney. The purpose of the letter is to provide a status report when serving the Notification. Typically, the letter will outline the terms of the trust regarding the distribution of assets- who will get what- and provide a rough timeline for the period of administration.

_____ 10. Lodge the original Will with the County Clerk, within 30 days of the date of death, pursuant to Probate Code §8500. Obtaining a copy of the Lodged Will may be necessary for the estate tax return (706), and lodging the Will is required by California law. Please note that California courts now impose a 'fee' of $50.00 for lodging the Will.

_____ 11. Submit the Certification of Trust and a Certified Death Certificate for each bank account and each brokerage account to be transferred. The Certification is prepared by the attorney. It is the document confirming your authority to act as Trustee. The bank or brokerage house may have its own form you will need to complete. The Certification from your attorney will include most or all of the information that is needed to complete the in-house certification.

CHAPTER EIGHTEEN
CHECKLIST WHEN REAL ESTATE IS PART OF THE TRUST ESTATE

REAL PROPERTY MATTERS

_____ 1. Prepare an Affidavit of Death of Trustee. Preparation, execution, and notarization of this document is necessary to remove the Trustmaker from title to the property and confirm you, as Trustee, as the 'legal' owner of the property so that you have the power and authority to deal with the property. You, as the representative of the Trust Estate, also have the liability associated with the property. That is why you should also confirm the property is insured.

_____ 2. Record the Affidavit of Death of Trustee with Certified Death Certificate attached. The Affidavit should be recorded in the county where the real property is located, together with a completed Preliminary Change of Ownership Report and any other documents required by that particular county for transmittal to the County Assessor's Office.

_____ 3. Prepare and send a Death of Real Property Owner Change in Ownership Statement to each county tax assessor where the decedent owned real property.

_____ 4. Prepare county specific forms for real estate. Each County in California has its own requirements for the forms it wants beyond the Affidavit and the Preliminary Ownership Report.

_____ 5. Prepare and file a Parent to Child Claim for Reassessment Exclusion, if applicable. If children are inheriting property from parents, the transfer of the primary residence plus an additional amount of other California real property (vacation homes, rental properties) can be accomplished *without reassessment of property taxes.* The importance of timely and proper filing of the Proposition 58 form is self-evident.

CHAPTER NINETEEN
CHECKLIST FOR DEALING WITH MISCELLANEOUS MATTERS IN THE ADMINISTRATION OF THE TRUST ESTATE

NOTIFICATIONS TO AGENCIES

_____ 1. Notify life insurance companies, file their "proof of loss" forms and collect proceeds.

_____ 2. If decedent had an IRA, 401K, pension and profit sharing plans, notify account holders and arrange for transfers to "roll-over IRA" for surviving spouse or other heirs.

_____ 3. Notify creditors for claims to be filed.

_____ 4. Notify Department of Health Services for any possible claims.

_____ 5. Contact State Controller regarding lost property.

_____ 6. Notify insurance companies for auto, homeowners and liability policies to advise of the passing of the Trustmaker.

TRANSFER OF ASSETS

_____ 1. Open a bank account in the Trustee's name as the successor Trustee of the trust, using the tax identification number obtained for the trust by the attorney or tax professional.

_____ 2. See to the distribution of personal property in roughly equivalent shares to all of the beneficiaries.

_____ 3. Transfer credit cards to name of surviving spouse, if desired, or close the account, if appropriate.

ESTATE TAXES

_____ 1. File decedent's final income tax return (Forms 1040 and 540).

_____ 2. Apply for federal taxpayer identification number for Bypass Trust, Marital Deduction or QTIP Trust, or Administrative Trust, if applicable.

_____ 3. Identify any lifetime gifts made by the decedent.

_____ 4. Provide attorney or accountant with all information gathered from the completion of the Chapter Seventeen and Chapter Eighteen checklists.

_____ 5. Prepare estate tax return (Form 706), which is due nine months after date of death. There is one six month extension available. Taxes are due nine months after date of death, even with an extension to file the estate tax return. Alternate valuation at six months after death can be elected.

_____ 6. File basis forms, if needed.

_____ 7. File trust income tax return (Forms 1041 and 541) each year.

DISTRIBUTE

_____ 1. Provide an accounting to the beneficiaries.

_____ 2. Pay creditors.

_____ 3. Distribute assets to beneficiaries and/or various sub-trusts as specified in the trust.

_____ 4. If spouse is surviving, allocate assets into Survivor's Trust, Marital Deduction or QTIP Trust, and Bypass Trust, based on the estate tax return and advice from the attorney or accountant.

CHAPTER TWENTY
DIVISION OF TASKS BETWEEN THE TRUSTEE, THE ATTORNEY, AND THE TAX PROFESSIONAL DURING THE ADMINISTRATION OF THE TRUST ESTATE

TRUSTEE'S TASKS VS. ATTORNEY'S TASKS

The accountant should and usually does prepare the taxes. However, tasks may be divided between the Trustee and attorney based on individual circumstances, which may change in every case. Below are examples of the usual division of tasks between the Trustee and the attorney.

ATTORNEY

- Writes to the beneficiaries of the trust outlining status and the further handling of the post mortem administration.

- Prepares and serves the Notification by Trustee.

- Obtains a tax identification number for the estate, and/ or the sub-trusts.

- Prepares the Affidavit of Death of Trustee, and county specific forms, for the Trustee's signature.

- Obtains an appraisal on the real property.

- Prepares Parent to Child Claim for Reassessment Exclusion form(s).

- Prepares spreadsheets for the trust accounting.

TRUSTEE

- Opens a bank account in the Trustee's name as the successor Trustee of the trust using the tax identification number obtained.

- Identifies all assets of the estate, and obtains date of death values for all bank/brokerage/investment accounts and estimates the value of personal property.

- Sees to the distribution of personal property in roughly equivalent shares to all of the beneficiaries.

- Keeps updated the spreadsheets provided by the attorney to account for all income and expenses associated with the Survivor's Trust, Marital Deduction or QTIP Trust, and Bypass Trust.

- Contacts the insurers for the real property to advise of the passing of the Trustmaker.

- Consolidates assets in the trust into one or two accounts for distribution.

CHAPTER TWENTY ONE
FINAL THOUGHTS FOR A TRUSTEE

The following points will help make your job easier, and they will help you avoid conflict with beneficiaries.

TRY TO UNDERSTAND WHY THE TRUST WAS CREATED

Understanding the intent behind the trust will help you fulfill your role as Trustee. There are many reasons for creating trusts, and there was probably more than one reason for creating this trust. Getting the drafting attorney to provide you with this information, even if you must pay for his or her time, can be invaluable to you later. Additionally, look for other written documents that may be incorporated into the trust or provide explanations behind the purpose of the trust. Most people who take the time to do estate planning are trying to protect and provide for their loved ones.

EXAMINE YOUR MOTIVES

You should be extremely careful that everything you do or refrain from doing as Trustee is motivated by your desire to execute your duties faithfully and to the best of your ability. You cannot allow yourself to be influenced by your personal feelings about individual beneficiaries or your own self-interest.

WHAT IF YOU ARE A BENEFICIARY OF THE TRUST?

As a beneficiary, you are entitled to benefit from the trust. However, it is critical that you remain impartial and faithfully carry out your duties to the other beneficiaries. If anything you do as Trustee smells of greed or self-interest, you will have a very difficult time convincing a judge or a jury that you satisfied your obligations as Trustee. If you are ever in doubt as to whether a conflict exists between your personal interests and those of other beneficiaries, it is better to abstain from acting until you have consulted your legal counsel, or, in appropriate cases, have received instructions from the court.

KEEP WELL-DOCUMENTED FILES

What should be in your trust files? In addition to your accountings, and the back-up information upon which your accountings are based, your files should include:

Notes from regular meeting with the beneficiaries

For each meeting, keep a record of the date, the length of the meeting, and a summary of what was discussed. You should also keep records of all other communications between you and the beneficiaries, including such things as copies of all correspondence.

A diary of your time devoted to Trustee tasks

You may or may not charge fees for your services. Whether or not you end up charging fees, a written record of the time devoted to your Trustee duties is good evidence that you fulfilled your duties systematically and with due diligence. Good record keeping is very important.

Beneficiaries' income tax returns

If the trust instrument grants you discretion in making distributions to beneficiaries, their income tax returns can provide you a great deal of helpful information. Those returns are, after all, signed under penalty for perjury. Beneficiaries may be reluctant to share their income tax returns with you, but your request for that kind of information is not unduly intrusive—no more so than a bank asking for the same documentation before deciding whether to loan money.

Beneficiaries' annual budgets

If you have discretionary authority with respect to distributions, you may even want to help prepare budgets for the beneficiaries. This shows that you have carefully considered their needs relative to discretionary distributions.

Verification of out of pocket expenditures

Since you are entitled to reimbursement of all reasonable amounts you advance on behalf of the trust, keep copies of proof of payment such as canceled checks or receipts.

Communications with advisors

Keep all copies of all correspondence between yourself and your advisors, and always ask them to at least summarize any advice they give you in writing.

Any and all information upon which any exercise of discretion is based

That might include such things as beneficiaries' bank statements, credit card statements, pay stubs or other employment information, invoices, proposals, and any other information they give you to justify a request for a distribution.

Please keep in mind that the guidelines laid out in this manual are far from exhaustive. These guidelines are intended to alert you to your duties and to impress upon you the significance of your responsibilities. Never shrink from asking for legal or other professional advice. That advice may cost something in the short run, but the cost can be far less than it takes to fix a mistake later on. Remember that the trust will pay the reasonable costs associated with your obtaining advice, but you could end up paying out of your own pocket for your failure to secure advice when needed.

ALTERNATIVE TO CONSERVATORSHIP

CHAPTER ONE
OVERVIEW OF DUTIES OF THE INCAPACITY TRUSTEE AND AGENT ON POWER OF ATTORNEY

The administration of a trust will differ depending on whether you are administering the trust during the incapacity of a Trustmaker, or after the death of a Trustmaker. This chapter will address the duties of a Trustee in the event of a Trustmaker's incapacity.

How do you know if the Trustmaker is incapacitated?

The trust document will typically contain instructions for determining the Trustmaker's incapacity. Requirements may include a certification by one or two physicians that the Trustmaker is not capable of managing his or her financial affairs. The trust may also include instructions for the use of a disability panel, in which a group of the Trustmaker's family or friends is identified to come together and make an informal determination as to the Trustmaker's ability to manage his or her own affairs. If the trust calls for the use of a disability panel, you may still need a certification by a medical professional in order to utilize the Power of Attorney for Finances to gain control of any assets left out of the trust. Once a Trustmaker has been deemed incapacitated and unable to manage his or her own affairs, your role of successor Trustee will commence and you will be able to step in and begin managing the incapacitated Trustmaker's affairs.

Ensure ongoing care of the incapacitated Trustmaker

First, and most importantly, you will need to make sure the incapacitated Trustmaker is receiving quality care in a supportive environment. If you are named the Agent under the Advance Health Care Directive, you will give copies of the health care documents to the physicians and care facilities. If you are not the named agent, you will make sure the named agent is notified, and you may wish to offer help in notifying the relatives, friends, or employer.

Review the documents

As this manual notes, reviewing and understanding the terms of the Revocable Living Trust is essential to you fulfilling your obligations and duties as Trustee. If the trust calls for the appointment of co-Trustees upon the incapacity of the Trustmaker, you should notify your co-Trustee. You may also wish to notify the attorney who prepared the trust agreement, as the attorney may have particular insight into the trust document and the incapacitated Trustmaker's intent in preparing the estate plan. The attorney may also be able to address any initial questions you have regarding the administration during incapacity. You will also want to consult with an attorney to represent you as the Trustee, and to prepare documents you will need to gain control over the assets of the trust.

If you are the Agent under the Power of Attorney for Finances or the Advance Health Care Directive, you will need to review these documents as well. The Power of Attorney for Finances will identify what authority you will have over the incapacitated Trustmakers' finances and assets. The Advance Health Care Directive may or may not provide instructions regarding how the incapacitated Trustmaker wants to be medically taken care of in the event of incapacity, including whether palliative care or life sustaining treatment is desired and whether there are instructions for making anatomical gifts.

BECOME KNOWLEDGEABLE ABOUT THE FINANCES

To ready yourself for an ongoing administration during a period of incapacity, you will need to become familiar and educate yourself as to the incapacitated Trustmaker's ongoing expenses and anticipated additional expenses. This includes familiarizing yourself with the insurance, both medical and long term care insurance, as assuming the Trustmaker's insurance benefits will cover a certain procedure or facility, without first confirming such, may be a costly mistake. Additionally, you will need to know what are the assets of the estate, where are they located, and their current values. Knowing how the incapacitated Trustmaker is receiving income, how much the income is, and when the income is being paid, along with knowing the regular, ongoing expenses of the estate will help you to establish a budget.

TAKE CONTROL OF ASSETS

If all assets have been transferred to the trust, you will be able to step in as Trustee and manage the incapacitated Trustmaker's affairs quickly and easily. You will need to have a new Certification of Trust prepared by an attorney, which will confirm your authority to act as Trustee. Attached to this Certification will be either the physician's certificate of incapacity, or the disability panel's certification of incapacity. You will then take the Certification of Trust to each financial institution to have the accounts transferred to you as successor Trustee. The bank or brokerage house may have its own form you will need to complete. However, the Certification from your attorney will include most or all of the information that is needed to complete the in-house certification.

When you sign documents on behalf of the Trust, including checks, you should sign your name as "[*Your Name*], Trustee." When you sign documents on behalf of the incapacitated person, in your role as Agent under the Power of Attorney for Finances, you should sign your name as "[*Incapacitated Person's Name*], by [*Your Name*] as Power of Attorney *or* Attorney-in-Fact." By signing as "Trustee" or "Power of Attorney," you will not be held personally liable as long as the action you are taking is within the scope of your authority as Trustee or Agent under the Power of Attorney for Finances.

COORDINATE THE ROLES

In some instances, the Agents named under the Advance Health Care Directive, the Power of Attorney for Finances and the successor Trustee of the revocable living trust may be different. If this is the case, it is important to delineate and coordinate each person's responsibilities and roles in overseeing the care of the incapacitated Trustmaker. Although the Agent under the Advance Health Care Directive, the Agent under the Power of Attorney for Finances, and the successor Trustee of the Trust share the common goal of providing ongoing care and management for the incapacitated Trustmaker's well-being, there is a strong possibility for conflict.

For medical matters, it will be very important to coordinate between all three roles as health care can be very expensive and constitute the major portion of the incapacitated Trustmaker's monthly budget. Health care decisions and the quality of care and comfort of the incapacitated Trustmaker should take priority over expense budgeting concerns.

For financial matters, if there are assets that have not been transferred to the trust then the Agent under the Power of Attorney for Finances will be the only person able to access those assets. If you are not the named agent, you will need to notify the person identified in the Power of Attorney for Finances of the Trustmaker's incapacity, and you will need to work with that agent to administer and utilize the assets left out of the trust. This will include working together to determine and prepare a budget, to pay the expenses of the incapacitated Trustmaker, and to manage and invest the assets prudently for the benefit of the incapacitated Trustmaker. Additionally, you will need to work with the agent to prepare and file the incapacitated Trustmaker's individual tax returns, and manage any other legal matters that are outside of the trust. You will also want to work with the Agent under the Power of Attorney for Finances to transfer assets not already in the trust to the trust.

ADMINISTER FOR THE BENEFIT OF THE INCAPACITATED TRUSTMAKER

Unless the trust states otherwise, during the incapacity of a Trustmaker the assets are to continue to be managed and used for the benefit of the incapacitated Trustmaker. Accordingly, your primary concern should be to provide for the best care for the incapacitated Trustmaker given the extent of assets available for the benefit of the Trustmaker. However, if there are minors or other dependents, the trust may identify that these dependents are to be provided for by the trust assets as well as the incapacitated Trustmaker. In this case, the trust will typically identify a priority for distributions of trust assets first to the incapacitated Trustmaker and then to the dependents.

In administering the trust for the benefit of the incapacitated Trustmaker, you will need to consider your fiduciary duty as successor Trustee. The elements of that duty are discussed in further detail later in this book. Additionally, you will likely want review and complete portions of the checklists found in the preceding chapters.

WHAT HAPPENS IF THE INCAPACITATED TRUSTMAKER RECOVERS?

If the incapacitated Trustmaker recovers and regains capacity, you will relinquish the role of acting Trustee, the Trustmaker will resume taking care of his or her own affairs, and you may remain named as a future successor Trustee in the event of incapacity or death of the Trustmaker.

EXECUTORS AND THE PROBATE PROCESS

CHAPTER ONE
PROBATE OVERVIEW

If you have agreed to act as the Executor of an estate, you should know that probate is an onerous, expensive and public procedure. Statutory probate fees are at 4% for the first $100,000 of assets subject to probate, 3% for the next $100,000, 2% for the next $800,000, and 1% on amounts over $1,000,000. These amounts are usually increased if the estate contains real property, and the fees are granted to each the attorney and Executor. The average probate takes 15 months, depending on the size of the estate and whether a federal estate tax return is required. The amount of time can be lengthier in cases involving disputes and/or litigation. It can also be shorter if things go smoothly. Additionally, unless the court is specially petitioned, the last to receive a distribution from the probate process are the persons the decedent wanted to benefit- the beneficiaries or heirs of the estate.

The probate process is commenced by filing the Probate Petition with the court. The court then sets a date for the hearing of the Probate Petition. When the court grants the petition, it will sign an order appointing you as the Executor of the Estate. You will want to request certified copies of the order and "Letters Testamentary" for the tasks you will be completing. The Letters

Testamentary is the document that will give you the legal authority to act on behalf of the estate.

The next step will be to marshal estate assets and complete an Inventory and Appraisal form, which then needs to be forwarded to the Probate Referee to value the assets. Also, any known creditors need to be served with the Notice of Probate. The creditors have four months from the issuance of Letters Testamentary to file a creditor's claim. The Executor then has to approve or reject the claim(s).

As a legal duty, one year after Letters Testamentary are issued, or 18 months if federal estate tax return is required, the Executor is required to file a Petition for Final Distribution. The court then sets a hearing date during which the Petition is approved if there are no outstanding issues or problems. Once the Petition is approved, the assets of the estate can be distributed.

The following diagram summarizes the probate process:

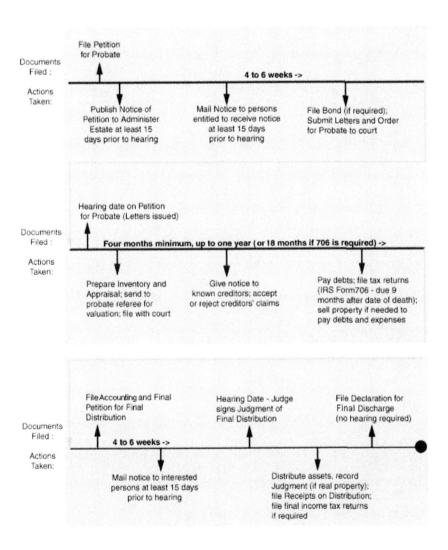

Documents
Filed :

File Petition
for Probate

4 to 6 weeks ->

Actions
Taken:

Publish Notice of
Petition to Administer
Estate at least 15
days prior to hearing

Mail Notice to persons
entitled to receive notice
at least 15 days
prior to hearing

File Bond (if required);
Submit Letters and Order
for Probate to court

Documents
Filed :

Hearing date on Petition
for Probate (Letters issued)

Four months minimum, up to one year (or 18 months if 706 is required) ->

Actions
Taken:

Prepare Inventory and
Appraisal; send to
probate referee for
valuation; file with court

Give notice to
known creditors; accept
or reject creditors' claims

Pay debts; file tax returns
(IRS Form706 - due 9
months after date of death);
sell property if needed to
pay debts and expenses

Documents
Filed :

File Accounting and Final
Petition for Final
Distribution

Hearing Date - Judge
signs Judgment of
Final Distribution

File Declaration for
Final Discharge
(no hearing required)

4 to 6 weeks ->

Actions
Taken:

Mail notice to interested
persons at least 15 days
prior to hearing

Distribute assets, record
Judgment (if real property);
file Receipts on Distribution;
file final income tax returns
if required

CHAPTER TWO
THE PROBATE PROCESS IN DETAIL

As the Executor of the estate, you will have a fiduciary duty to the estate and the beneficiaries of the estate. The summary of your duties and responsibilities are as follows:

- Make prudent investments on behalf of the estate. Prudent investment means investing with the care of a prudent person dealing with someone else's property; given that the time period of the probate is relatively short, preservation of principal should be stressed. Therefore, federally insured savings accounts and/or Certificates of Deposit in denominations of less than $100,000 are suggested. Except for a checking account, all other estate accounts must earn interest;

- Keep estate assets separate from personal assets or any other person's assets; and

- Spend estate money only when necessary to cover the estate debts or costs associated with the estate and administration of the estate.

SUMMARY OF YOUR TASKS AS EXECUTOR

Your 3 primary tasks as Executor of the estate may be summarized as follows:

- Identify and marshal all of the estate assets;

- Value the assets; and

- Distribute the assets pursuant to the terms of the estate plan, which is controlled by the Will or the rules of intestate succession.

A more detailed list includes:

- Locate the decedent's assets and manage them during the probate process;

- Receive payments due to the estate, including interest, dividends, and other income;

- Set up an estate bank account to hold money that is owed to the decedent, such as paychecks or stock dividends;

- Ascertain who is going to get what and how much;

- Value or appraise the estate's assets, which is done for the most part by the Probate Referee. You may value cash assets;

- Give official legal notice to creditors and potential creditors of the probate proceeding and the deadlines for creditors to file claims according to state law;

- Investigate the validity of all claims against the estate;

- Pay funeral bills, outstanding debts, and valid claims;

- Use estate funds to pay continuing expenses, such as mortgage payments, utility bills and homeowner's insurance premiums;

- Handle day-to-day details, such as disconnecting utilities, ending leases and cancelling credit cards, and notifying banks and government agencies (Social Security, the post office, etc.);

- File tax returns and pay income and estate taxes. This will including a final State and Federal income tax return covering the period from the beginning of the tax year to the date of death;

- After getting the court's permission, distribute the decedent's property to the decedent's beneficiaries; and

- File receipts for distribution and wrap up any closing details for the estate.

YOUR AUTHORITY TO ACT AND INFORMATION ON OPENING A BANK ACCOUNT

The "Letters Testamentary" is the document that gives you authority to act as the Executor or Administrator of the estate. This document, along with a copy of the tax identification number, is what is needed to open accounts in the name of the estate. When you sign documents on behalf of the estate including checks, you should sign your name as "[*Your Name*], Executor," or "[*Your Name*], Administrator," depending on how you hold this position as identified in the Letters Testamentary.

By signing as "Executor" or "Administrator," you will not be held personally liable as long as the action you are taking is within the scope of your authority as Executor or Administrator for the estate.

As soon as the Letters Testamentary is issued, it would be best to consolidate all accounts into a single estate account under your name as Executor. The account will have its own tax identification number, which will need to be obtained upon receipt of the Letters Testamentary. The account will act as an administrative account where all income will be placed and all expenses will be paid. It is also the account from which distributions to beneficiaries will be made. Generally speaking, the account will have two sub accounts, a savings account and a checking account. At the start of the administration, most money should be accumulated in the savings account so that the estate will be earning income during the pendency of the probate. As bills need to be paid, you will want to transfer funds to the checking account and write checks to the payees.

MARSHALING AND VALUING ASSETS

Once the probate process is started, you will first need to identify and locate all assets held by the decedent at the time of their death. This includes personal property (furniture, furnishings, jewelry, etc.), and any bank or brokerage accounts. Please note that gifts of personal property to charity should be reasonably valued and documented as the estate can deduct the same.

All assets are to be valued based on the *date of death* value of each asset. The Probate Referee will value the real property; hence, you do not need to concern yourself with obtaining an appraisal of the real property.

While the final value of personal property is determined by the Probate Referee, you need to provide the Referee with information on the personal property and an estimate you make. In this regard, you should consider the following scenario: all personal property (furniture, furnishings, clothing, silverware, jewelry, art, bric-a-brac, etc.) is placed on the driveway on Saturday morning for an estate sale. The sale closes down on Sunday afternoon and any remaining property is given to a charity. The question is, how much would be in the cash box. This is the amount that should be identified as the date of death value for the personal property. If there is any substantive personal property, such as collectibles or more expensive jewelry, this should be listed separately with an appraised value.

The Inventory and Appraisal Form will be filed with the Probate Referee to value the estate assets. You need to provide a complete list of all properties, bank accounts, cars, brokerage accounts and the like that were owned by the decedent at the time of his or her death. You will also include an estimate of the value of the decedent's personal property for the purpose of filing this form. Generally, all personal property is valuated as a single item, and stated as a lump sum under the heading "personal property".

PAYING DEBTS AND LIABILITIES OF THE ESTATE

Please keep detailed records with regard to monies moving in and out of the estate. Please remember that as the Executor of the estate, you are charged with a fiduciary obligation to the beneficiaries. In other words, the relationship you have as Executor is the same as the relationship an attorney has with his or her clients. You are obligated under the law to marshal assets, invest those assets prudently and distribute those assets. As you can see, your obligations are substantial. **The best way to fulfill your**

obligation is to keep track of where funds are coming from and where those funds are going to. Good record keeping usually saves a good deal of problems in the future.

Also, as there may be extraordinary time and expenses associated with your role as Executor. You should therefore keep a diary of the time you devote to the administration of the estate. The diary should be a contemporaneous log you keep of activities performed, and costs and expenses advanced, on behalf of the estate. Please note the date, the time spent and the activity for each item. This should be kept in a separate calendar, log or binder which can be copied in the event the court requests additional documentation on an item at some point in the future.

Estate tax return

An estate tax return (Form 706) may or may not need to be filed based on the total value of the estate as of the date of death and the estate tax exemption available to the decedent in the year he or she died. If an estate tax return is necessary, the return, or a request for an extension, will be due in nine months of the date of death. One six-month extension may be obtained on the estate tax return. However, the estate tax (if any) is due nine months from the date of death, regardless of an extension for filing of the return.

Income tax returns

There is a "bright line" separating time before the date of death from time after the date of death. A final income tax return (Forms 1040 and 540) will need to be filed for the decedent, which will recognize income and deductions available to the decedent up to the date of his or her death. From the date of death forward, income and deductions are chargeable to the estate and an estate income tax return (Forms 1041 and 541) may be necessary.

DISTRIBUTION OF ASSETS

The distribution of the estate assets will depend on the complexity of the estate. In preparing for distributions, you will want to provide an accounting of the estate. This accounting differs from an income tax accounting. The accounting requires you to identify all assets at the beginning of the accounting period (the date of death) and track those assets up to and through the date of distribution. You will be responsible for showing all income earned by the estate, all expenses paid by the estate, and all disbursements from estate assets. Accordingly, consolidation of estate assets into as few accounts as possible is recommended to make this process a more simple one. It is easier to track income on one or two accounts than on several accounts. If the decedent's beneficiaries agree to waive the accounting, there will be no need to complete a formal accounting. Otherwise, you will work on a formal accounting to include with the final petition to the court.

Once an account is prepared, or waived by the beneficiaries, and all other steps have been completed in the administration process, the estate will be ready for distribution. You will then prepare and file a Final Petition for Distribution with the court, to document the completion of the administration steps and to obtain court confirmation of the distribution of the estate assets to the respective beneficiaries. Upon approval of the final petition, and once the distributions are made, you will obtain receipts from each beneficiary confirming the distributions were completed. You will also file an Ex Parte Petition for Final

Discharge and Order to release you of any ongoing administrative duties or obligations to the estate.

Overall difficulties with probate

Let's face it, probate in the State of California can be an expensive and onerous process. The probate process comes out of the middle ages and was designed, in part, to assure the creditors (that is the King) got their share of the estate before the beneficiaries received anything.

Probate fees to be charged by the Executor and the attorney are set by California Statute, and extraordinary fees can be added to that amount. There are numerous technical requirements and various court costs that will tend to vex persons untrained in the process and slow the estate administration. It will take, on average, 15 months before a final distribution is ordered by the court, and there is necessary follow up with the court after the estate is actually distributed to formally close out the probate estate.

In short, probate is a process to be avoided.

WHAT ABOUT PLANNING
FOR MY ESTATE?

CHAPTER ONE
THE BASIC PLANNING OPTIONS

Don't have an Estate plan? California has one for you-
It is called Intestate Succession and you had better
watch out!

In California, when a person dies without a plan in place that person dies "intestate". In that instance, the State of California has set forth rules to determine who are the heirs that will inherit the estate, or the "heirs at law". These rules are known as the rules of intestate succession.

To determine the heirs at law, one must answer a series of questions about the decedent. These questions include whether the decedent was married, if they had children, and if there were any other surviving members of the decedent's family. Below are two illustrations outlining how the answers to these questions may affect the heirs at law, as determined by the rules of intestate succession.

Unmarried

John, a resident of California, died without a Will or Living Trust. He was not married at the time of his death. In this instance, John's estate will be distributed as follows:

a) To John's children, who take in equal shares. If John has surviving grandchildren from a predeceased child, the predeceased child's share will be divided equally between those grandchildren.

b) If there are no children or other living issue (i.e. children, grandchildren, great-grandchildren, etc.), John's estate will go to his parents.

c) If John's parents are not alive, the estate will go to the issue of his parents. In other words, if John had siblings, his estate will be divided equally between his living brothers and sisters. If John was predeceased by a sibling, who has surviving children, that sibling's share will be divided equally between the living children. If John was predeceased by all his siblings, his estate will be divided equally between his nieces and nephews.

d) If John was not survived by his parents, siblings, nieces or nephews, then John's estate will go to his grandparents.

e) If there are no surviving grandparents, John's estate will be inherited by the issue of his grandparents, which may ultimately include aunts, uncles, or cousins.

f) In the event that John was not survived by any family members, then his entire estate will escheat (be turned over) to the State of California.

In the end, if you die unmarried and without a plan in place, your estate will travel through your family tree, will find the closest living blood relative to you, and will distribute at that level. Again, if there is no surviving blood relative, then the entire estate will revert to the State of California.

Married

Dean, a resident of California, died without a Will or Living Trust. However, Dean was married at the time of his death. In this instance, we must first ask what is the character of Dean's property in order to determine who will inherit his property.

There are two types of property in California, community property and separate property. Community property may be generally defined as those assets earned or acquired during the marriage. Separate property may be generally defined as those assets brought into the marriage, assets received by inheritance, or assets received by gift. It is important to note that these are generalized definitions. California case law in fact provides many exceptions to these generalizations, including the change in character of an asset from separate property to community property, or vice versa.

After identifying the character of the assets in the estate, Dean's estate will be distributed as follows:

a. Community Property

i   All community property will pass to Dean's spouse, who may file a spousal property petition with the Court to establish ownership.

b. Separate Property

i   Dean's surviving spouse will receive all of his separate property, if he is not survived by issue, parents, siblings, or children of deceased siblings.

ii Dean's surviving spouse will receive 1/2 of his separate property, if Dean was survived by only one child, or issue of a deceased child. The other 1/2 of Dean's separate property will go to the surviving child, or the surviving issue of his deceased child.

iii Dean's surviving spouse will receive 1/2 of his separate property, if Dean had no surviving children but was survived by parents, siblings, or children of deceased siblings. The other 1/2 of Dean's separate property will be distributed to the first living generation starting with his parents, then his siblings, then his nieces and nephews.

iv Dean's surviving spouse will receive 1/3 of his separate property, if Dean was survived by more than one child, or by one child and the issue of one or more deceased children. The other 2/3 of Dean's separate property will be distributed to the surviving children, or 1/3 to the surviving child and 1/3 to the surviving issue of one or more deceased children.

v   Dean's surviving spouse will receive 1/3 of his separate property, if Dean was survived by the issue of two or more deceased children. The other 2/3 of Dean's separate property will be distributed to the surviving issue of his deceased children.

As you can see, the intent of California's rules of intestate succession are to provide for distribution of assets to the closest living blood relatives, even if those relatives are people you may never have had any contact with. However, all of the above considerations may be made irrelevant if you put an estate plan in place yourself, either through a Will or Living Trust.

PLANNING FOR AFTER DEATH ONLY WITH A LAST WILL AND TESTAMENT

As noted previously in this manual, a Will is not a living document. Though signed today, the Will does not speak until after your death. However, a Will, or Last Will and Testament, is meant to direct your assets pursuant to your wishes, therefore giving you the peace of mind that your assets will be distributed to your intended beneficiaries.

Unlike the rules of intestate succession, in a Last Will and Testament you will call out those individuals to which you wish to benefit from your estate after your death. Depending on your wishes, the beneficiaries to your Will may include your spouse, domestic partner, children, relatives, friends, charitable organizations, or even state or governmental entities. For these beneficiaries, you will identify what fraction or percentage of your estate will pass to each of them upon your death. You may even identify a specific piece of property or asset that you wish to pass to one or more beneficiaries directly.

Furthermore, in a Last Will and Testament you will also identify the person you wish to act as the executor of your estate and who will be the person responsible for carrying out the Will's instructions.

For those individuals with children under the age of 18, the Last Will and Testament will identify who you wish to serve as the legal guardian of your child(ren), and who will manage any property left to your minor child(ren) through your Will.

Exceptions to assets passing by Will

A Last Will and Testament is designed to control the distribution of all assets owned in one's individual name at the time of their death. Accordingly, there are certain assets that will not be subject to the distribution plan outlined in the Will.

- Retirement Plans. The funds remaining in retirement plans (401K, IRA, etc.) are directed through beneficiary designations. Only if a retirement plan is left without a beneficiary designation, will the plan be subject to the terms of your Last Will and Testament.

- Life Insurance. Similar to retirement plans, proceeds from life insurance policies are directed through beneficiary designations. Again, only if a policy is left without a beneficiary designation, will the proceeds be subject to the terms of the Last Will and Testament.

- "Pay on Death" or "Transfer on Death" Accounts. These accounts generally have an individual, or individuals, named as beneficiaries to these accounts upon the death of the account holder.

- Living Trusts. Assets that are titled to a Living Trust will be distributed pursuant to the terms of the trust.

Preparing a Will

There are several basic requirements for preparing and imple- menting a valid Last Will and Testament in California. The foremost requirements include being 18 years or older, and being of sound mind with the capability for making decisions and reasoning. Once these initial requirements are met, there are form requirements for the document including being in writing and signed by the person making the Will, the conservator for the person under a Court order, or someone on the person's behalf who executes the document in that person's presence and under their direction. Finally, a true Last Will and Testament must be witnessed by two independent persons who are present at the time the Will is executed.

If not all requirements are met for a Last Will and Testament, the courts in California will also recognize a holographic Will. A holographic Will is one that is handwritten, legible, and signed. The courts will also recognize a California Statutory Will, which is a template or "fill-in-the-blank" form for those individuals with small and simple estates.

Changing and revoking a Will

A benefit to preparing and implementing a Will is that it may be changed whenever you desire. In fact, it is recommended that you review your Will periodically, and update the terms to address any changes in circumstances or intentions. To change a Will, you may execute a codicil amending the terms of your original Last Will and Testament. The same formalities for preparing and implementing the original Will also apply to preparing and implementing a codicil.

In the event the terms of your Will have dramatically changed, or you simply wish to start over, the revocation of your Will may be accomplished by expressly revoking all or a part of the document in a subsequent Will. However, this may very well lead to potential disputes in court after your death. For instance, should you remove a beneficiary from your distribution plan in a subsequent Will, that beneficiary may raise a claim that you did not have proper capacity to have executed the subsequent document, and therefore the first document should be applied to the estate. In order to prevent potential disputes, a Will may also be revoked by being canceled, torn, burned, obliterated or otherwise destroyed by you with the intent and for the purpose of revocation of the document. This may also be done by someone else, in your presence and so directed by yourself.

Planning for incapacity and after death with a Revocable Living Trust

At death, a Revocable Living Trust and a Will have the same basic goal, to distribute an estate pursuant to the specific instructions and wishes of the decedent. With both documents, the decedent is planning with intention. However, there are significant differences between Will based and Revocable Living Trust based planning. These differences include whether or not assets will be subject to probate, and how assets will be managed during an individual's incapacity.

Avoiding probate

One of the significant advantages to the use of a Revocable Living Trust in California is the ability to avoid probate on all assets that you title to your living trust. As described earlier in this manual, probate can be a time consuming process. Because probate is a court directed process, the proceedings are governed by the court's calendar. An average probate can take between 15 to 18 months. Additionally, a probate can become very expensive for the estate. In a probate, the attorney and Executor are each awarded statutory fees based upon the gross value of the estate. These fees are calculated at 4% of the first $100,000, 3% of the next $100,000, 2% of the next $800,000, and 1% of the next $9,000,000. As an example, the statutory fees on a $1,000,000 estate equal $23,000 for the attorney and $23,000 for the Executor. Furthermore, there is generally no privacy in probate proceedings, as the probate process is a matter of public record.

Through the use of a living trust, you will forego the probate process and your named successor Trustees will informally manage and distribute your assets on your behalf, and with a level of privacy that court proceedings simply do not afford. Furthermore, a Revocable Living Trust provides you with the most control over your assets, as the document provides for instructions on managing those assets for your benefit if you are incapacitated or unable to manage them on your own behalf.

Maintaining and maximizing control

A common myth about trusts is that, once the assets are titled to the trust you lose some amount of control over them. However, for a Revocable Living Trust the very opposite is true. Though title to your assets will change from you as an individual to you as Trustee of your trust, by being the Trustmaker to the trust you retain full control over those assets. This means that you can put assets into the trust or take them out at any time, you can change the character of the assets, and you can change the terms of the trust at any time. Essentially, while you are alive and well *you are your trust.*

Unlike a Will, A Revocable Living Trust allows you to provide instructions to your successor Trustee for the management of your assets during your incapacity. The trust is designed to provide for an efficient transition in control to your successor Trustee, should you become unable to manage the trust assets yourself. Additionally, instructions in the trust provide that the assets are to continue to be used for your benefit. The incapacity instructions, depending on the level of detail provided, may even go so far as to provide protection for your successor Trustees from the possible interference of Adult Protective Services.

Finally, when creating your Revocable Living Trust you provide specific instructions regarding who is to receive your assets and how they may receive them. You may wish to include instructions that provide for distributions at certain ages or milestones, or include instructions for maintenance of inherited funds in lifetime, irrevocable trusts that can provide for a beneficiary over their lifetime with certain protections.

Estate tax considerations

There is no inheritance or estate tax currently imposed by the State of California. However, in 2013 the federal government imposed a permanent Federal Estate Tax on estates in excess of $5 million. This figure was indexed for inflation, and as of 2017 the exemption has increased to $5.49 million per person. For married couples, a Revocable Living Trust may help you to avoid taxes if your total estate is over the exemption by including instructions for the division of assets into sub-trusts at the death of the first spouse. These sub-trusts are often referred to as an A/B/C trust split, and include various synonyms such as: Survivor's Trust, Marital Trust, Exemption Trust, Bypass Trust, QTIP Trust, etc. With this sub-trust planning, assets will pass to the surviving spouse through these sub-trusts while providing for estate tax savings at the same time. The use of sub-trust planning in a Revocable Living Trust involves various technical considerations, and it is recommended you seek legal counsel to discuss the advantages and disadvantages to the sub-trust planning in further detail.

Preparing a Revocable Living Trust

A living trust is a legal contract that establishes the trust, and details how the trust will be managed and distributed. Similar to preparing a Will, the foremost requirements for preparing a trust include being 18 years or older, and having capacity. The trust must also be in writing, be signed by the Trustmaker (also known as Grantor or Settlor), and be notarized.

While a Will is effective upon execution, a trust is only effective once assets are titled to the trust. Titling assets to a trust is often referred to as "funding" the trust. In funding your trust, you will transfer the title to your assets from yourself as an individual, to yourself as Trustee of the trust. It should be a priority to transfer title of your assets to your living trust once the trust is established, as any assets left outside of the trust may be subject to probate upon your death.

Exceptions to assets passing by Revocable Living Trust

Similar to a Will based plan, there are certain assets that will not be immediately titled to your living trust, or may not ever be governed by the instructions in your living trust.

- Retirement Plans. The funds remaining in retirement plans (401K, IRA, etc.) are directed through beneficiary designations. If you were to change title to the retirement plan immediately to the trust, this would be considered a change in ownership and all the deferred taxes would become due. Should you wish for your retirement plan to be managed and distributed pursuant to the terms of your Revocable Living Trust, you may name the trust as a designated beneficiary of the plan.

- Life Insurance. Similar to retirement plans, proceeds from life insurance policies are directed through beneficiary designations. Again, should you wish for a payout from a life insurance policy to be managed and distributed pursuant to the terms of your Revocable Living Trust, you may name the trust as a designated beneficiary of the policy.

- "Pay on Death" or "Transfer on Death" Accounts. These accounts generally have an individual, or individuals, named as beneficiaries to these accounts upon your death.

What is best for you?

Even if you are a person of modest means, you have worked hard to earn your money and preserve your assets. Everyone who owns assets, be it through a bank account, brokerage account, real property, etc., has an estate. By reading the foregoing discussions, you are now familiar with the several strategies available for ensuring your assets are managed and distributed according to your wishes. While a Will based plan may be a more cost conscious strategy to implement now, the future savings from the efficient management of your assets during your incapacity and the avoidance of probate after your death may make the additional investment for the preparation of a Revocable Living Trust worthwhile.

However, choosing which strategy to implement depends entirely on your individual circumstances. A plan that might be right for one family may not be right for everyone. Consulting with a competent attorney about your individual family's needs and concerns can help you make the right decision for yourself, your family, and your future.

CHAPTER TWO
THE ESTATE PLANNING ROADMAP

THE WHO'S WHO OF AN ESTATE PLAN

Whether you elect to implement a Will based or a Revocable Living Trust based estate plan, it is important to identify the right persons to fill the various roles in these plans. As discovered earlier in this manual, the roles being filled in an estate plan ultimately determine how efficiently the estate will be administered either during incapacity or after death. Picking the right Executor, Trustee, or agents can help ensure the prompt, accurate, and efficient management of assets during incapacity, and distribution of assets after death.

The Trustmaker

The person entering into the trust agreement, and establishing the trust based estate plan. This role is also referred to as the Grantor, Settlor, and Trustor.

The Trustee

The role of Trustee is one of the most important roles to identify in a Revocable Living Trust. A successor Trustee is one who will step into the role of managing the trust in the event that you decide to hand over this responsibility to another person as you age. The successor Trustee will also automatically step into the management position in the event of your incapacity or death.

Serving as a successor Trustee is a fiduciary responsibility, which can require a significant amount of time and effort on behalf of the person named in that position. The ideal candidate for this role is someone who is honest, dependable, an effective communicator, well-organized, good with paperwork, and capable of meeting deadlines. A family member or close friend who meets most of these criteria may be a great choice for serving in this role.

Depending on the size of the estate, the complexity of the instructions provided in the trust, or interfamilial issues, a corporate or private professional Trustee may be another great choice for serving in this role. A corporate Trustee is generally a bank trust department or trust company, whereas a private professional Trustee is generally an individual fiduciary or group of individual fiduciaries. Both a corporate Trustee and private professional Trustee will bring with them a level of experience, objectivity and professional resources to manage the assets in the trust and ensure that the trust is being administered and distributed in an unbiased manner and pursuant to the terms outlined. However, the increased knowledge and experience that a professional brings to the role comes with additional expense. A professional Trustee will likely charge a higher hourly rate, or percentage of the estate as Trustee fees than would a friend or family member as Trustee fees. Before naming a professional

Trustee, it is recommended that you interview the professionals you are considering naming in order to fully understand their services and fees.

The Executor

Similar to the role of Trustee, the Executor in a Will based estate plan serves as the primary role for the management and distribution of assets after death. The Executor serves in a fiduciary capacity, and is responsible for the efficient and proper distribution of assets pursuant to the terms of the Will. As such, the ideal candidate is again someone who is honest, dependable, an effective communicator, well-organized, good with paperwork, and capable of meeting deadlines.

The Guardian

When you have a child under the age of 18, a guardian should be named to care for that child in the event of both parents' death. Guardians will be named regardless as to whether the estate plan is trust based or Will based. Without naming a guardian, the determination as to who will care for the child will be left entirely up to the court and strangers; and one should not assume that the court will automatically grant custody to grandparents, aunts, uncles, or even other family members.

Considerations to keep in mind when nominating a guardian include:

- How many children do you have under the age of 18?

- Do you prefer that all of your children to live together?

- How old is the nominated guardian, and can they physically and financially manage all of your children?

- Where is the nominated guardian located, and how would potential relocation affect your children?

- How would the nominated guardian raise your children, and would that be consistent with your personal and religious values and ideals?

Nominating a guardian is a highly personal and sensitive topic for parents. However, one of the most important parts of your job as a parent is to ensure that your children are cared for in the event you are no longer able to care for them yourself. By taking the time to carefully consider the factors listed above, you will be able to make the best choice possible for your children.

The Power of Attorney for Finances Agent

The Power of Attorney for Finances is a legal document that grants authority to agents to act on a person's behalf in the event they are alive but not well enough to manage their own financial and legal affairs. This role is similar to the role of Trustee, however agents under a Power of Attorney for Finances act with regard to any asset held in an individual capacity and not held as Trustee, or with regard to any legal matters against someone individually.

Depending upon how the document is worded, a Power of Attorney for Finances may become immediately effective upon signing, or may become effective upon some future event such as incapacity. Typically, spouses will be named as a primary agent and may serve effective immediately upon signing. However, due to the powerful nature of this document, it is recommended that, for any agents named who are not spouses, the power become effective only upon incapacity of the principal (the one signing the document). Additionally, the powers conferred through the Power of Attorney for Finances end upon the death of the principal.

There are only two legal requirements for naming an agent on the Power of Attorney for Finances, that the agent be at least 18 years old and have capacity. However, the agents named in this document may be made responsible for numerous financial matters at the election of the principal, including:

- Real property transactions;

- Tangible personal property transactions;

- Stock and bond transactions;

- Commodity and option transactions;

- Banking and other financial institution transactions;

- Business operating transactions;

- Insurance and annuity transactions;

- Estate, trust and other beneficiary transactions;

- Claims and litigation;

- Personal and family maintenance;

- Benefits from social security, Medicare, Medicaid, or other governmental programs, or civil or military service;

- Retirement plan transactions; and

- Tax matters.

Due to the significant power held by an agent under a Power of Attorney for Finances, it is recommended that the nominated individual be trustworthy, honest, dependable, and well-organized. Often times the nominated successor Trustee(s) or Executor(s) will also be the nominated agent(s) on the Power of Attorney for Finances, due to the overlapping nature of these roles.

The Advance Health Care Directive Agent

The Advance Health Care Directive, or Healthcare Power of Attorney, is a legal document that grants agents authority to make medical decisions on your behalf in the event you are unable to make them for yourself. The Advance Health Care Directive also allows a person to make decisions for themselves as to whether they wish to receive life-sustaining support, or make anatomical gifts after their passing.

In nominating an agent to serve on your Advance Health Care Directive, considerations should include:

- How will this person react in potentially emotionally stressful and tense situations?

- Does this person know how your personal and religious values would impact treatment choices, even if this means you may die?

- Will this person take the initiative to advocate on your behalf with regard to hospital staff, doctors, surgeons, etc.?

- Where is this person located, will they be easily reached by emergency personnel, and will they be able to travel in an emergency if necessary?

Once a primary agent and backup agents are identified, it is a good idea to have a discussion with those agents to ensure they are aware your specific wishes if a medical emergency arises, and how best they can serve as an advocate on your behalf. Additionally, it is important to provide a copy of the Advance Health Care Directive to your named agents, so they may provide proof of authority to act on your behalf in the event of a medical emergency.

The HIPAA Agent

HIPAA is an acronym that stands for the Health Insurance Portability and Accountability Act that was passed by Congress in 1996. The primary purpose for HIPAA was to give patients more control over their health information, and to set boundaries on the use and release of health records. When included in an estate plan, a HIPAA allows the principal to name individuals who will have rights to receive medical information pertaining to the principal. Ultimately, a HIPAA allows for the family members and friends' ability to communicate with medical professionals.

It is important to identify on the HIPAA the agents nominated on the Advance Health Care Directive, so they may receive medical information and make informed decisions on your behalf. However, while the Advance Health Care Directive authorizes the nominated agent to make medical decisions or advocate medically on a person's behalf, the agents named on the HIPAA have no power to make decisions on your behalf. A HIPAA only allows for gathering of medical information.

Accordingly, the HIPAA may also be an appropriate place to name family members or close friends who may not have met your personal considerations for being an agent on your Advance Health Care Directive. These persons will nevertheless be able to remain involved in your care, and will be able to contact the medical professionals to stay updated as to your status. This may be especially appropriate in the case where family members are not geographically local, and may not be able to travel easily.

Regardless as to who you name on the HIPAA release, it is recommended that the one executed document remain the only copy and in your possession until a medical emergency occurs. This is to protect your medical information and privacy, unless and until medical circumstances necessitate the release of information accordingly.

The What's What of an estate plan

Through intentional planning with the use of a Will or Revocable Living Trust, the estate may be directed to specific family members, friends, and even charities. When naming multiple beneficiaries to an estate, it is important to decide how the assets will be distributed among those beneficiaries. Common methods of distribution include:

- Equal distribution among all beneficiaries;

- Unequal distribution among beneficiaries (e.g. 75% to parents and 25% to siblings);

- Specific distributions of certain property or assets to certain beneficiaries;

- Distribution of a portion of the estate to be divided equally among a group of persons; and

- Distribution for the benefit and care of a beloved pet.

Additionally, when naming beneficiaries to an estate it is important to consider how the distributions may be made. For instance, if an estate consisting of one piece of real property is left equally to two children, what will happen if one child wants to sell the property and the other child does not. In an instance in which property is left with family heirlooms to multiple beneficiaries, the heirlooms may ultimately need to be sold to fairly distribute the value among those beneficiaries.

When should beneficiaries assume full responsibility?

There are many considerations to be made when determining the appropriate time for a beneficiary to assume full responsibility for their inheritance. A non-exhaustive list of considerations includes:

- Do you have specific concerns regarding the beneficiary being a spendthrift or having destructive habits?

- Is the beneficiary disabled?

- Is the beneficiary a minor?

- How large is the inheritance being left to this beneficiary?

Once these considerations are made, there are three basic options that may be utilized to address any specific concerns regarding beneficiaries.

Outright distribution

Depending on the size of the estate and the age of the beneficiary, an outright distribution may be the most appropriate and effective means of distributing assets. Through an outright distribution, once the property going to the beneficiary is identified the property will be given to that beneficiary immediately upon completion of the trust administration. This may be accomplished through a cash distribution, or through titling of property to the individual's name.

The beneficiary in an outright distribution plan will immediately assume full control over their inheritance, and will be able to do whatever he or she wishes with that inheritance.

Staged distribution

When the named beneficiaries to an estate are minors, or of younger ages, a staged distribution plan may be an appropriate means of prolonging distributions until the beneficiaries are at ages when they can make reasoned decisions. An example of a staged distribution plan is as follows

- At age 25, the beneficiary has the right to receive 1/3 of the principal of their share;

- At age 30, the beneficiary has the right to receive 1/2 of the remaining principal of their share; and

- At age 35, the beneficiary has the right to receive whatever principal remains of their share.

In this scenario, the beneficiary's share will remain held in trust for their benefit until they reach the identified ages. While the funds are held in trust, the beneficiary has the right to all of the income from their share, and they may even be allowed to request distributions of principal prior to reaching those ages for certain reasons such as health expenses or education expenses. Again, the purpose of a staged distribution plan is to prolong the time at which the beneficiaries will assume full control over their inheritance.

Lifetime trust distribution

A lifetime trust distribution plan is a more comprehensive and constrictive plan for distributing assets to beneficiaries. This planning is optimal in cases where the estate is of a significant size, or there are specific concerns regarding the inheriting beneficiary, such as disabilities, destructive behaviors, or spend-thrift behavior.

With a distribution of assets to a lifetime trust, the assets are held on behalf of the beneficiary for his or her lifetime. The beneficiary is entitled to receipt of the interest produced by the trust assets, and may be allowed to request distributions of principal for certain reasons such as health expenses, education expenses, maintenance or support. In the appropriate circumstances, at a certain age the beneficiary may become co-Trustee of their individual trust with another, and at a second age the beneficiary may become the sole Trustee of their individual trust. This allows a beneficiary time to learn how to manage the trust and assets prudently, while still ultimately allowing the beneficiary to one day assume total control of the management of the assets. However, if the beneficiary suffers from disabilities or destructive behaviors, an independent person may be named to manage the trust for that beneficiary's lifetime.

Through lifetime trusts there is also the benefit of creditor and predator protection. With lifetime trusts, the assets are owned by the trust for the benefit of the beneficiary, and the assets are not owned by the beneficiary individually. If the beneficiary is personally sued, he or she may lose all of his or her personal assets. However, the creditor will find it difficult to access the assets held in the lifetime trust. If the beneficiary goes through a divorce, again the beneficiary's individual assets will be subject to the divorce proceedings and division. However, the ex-spouse will find it difficult to access the assets held in the lifetime trust.

Finally, lifetime trust planning for beneficiaries provides an additional step of planning for inheritance through naming the successor beneficiaries to the remaining interest in the trust. When the primary beneficiary named to the lifetime trust dies, and there are remaining assets in the trust, a second beneficiary or group of beneficiaries may be identified to inherit the remaining assets. This ultimately provides the option of keeping assets in your bloodline, and ensuring ongoing support for future generations.

COMPLETING THE ROADMAP

As identified in this chapter, completing the roadmap for your individualized estate plan requires numerous considerations and personal choices. This process can be an emotional and daunting one, but is necessary in order to complete a plan that ensures your wishes are carried out after you are gone.

We have provided here an outline of non-exhaustive options and considerations for preparing your estate plan, and we recommend that you review these in further detail with an attorney to ensure the right decisions are made for you and your loved ones. An experienced attorney will be able to provide you with guidance and the peace of mind that your estate planning documents are prepared properly. So please do not wait. Knowing that you have a properly prepared plan formed and in place will give you and your family peace of mind, and may ultimately be one of the most thoughtful and considerate gifts you can give to yourself and the ones you love.

TERMS AND DEFINITIONS

A/B Trust Planning – A common planning technique used for a family trust when the estate has a value that exceeds the Trustmakers' remaining estate tax exemption amount. At the death of the first spouse, an "A Trust" is established for the benefit of the surviving spouse. This trust may more specifically be referred to as the Marital Trust or Survivor's Trust. Separately, a "B Trust" is established for the benefit of the surviving spouse and the deceased spouse's descendants. This trust may more specifically be referred to as the Bypass Trust, Exempt Trust, or Family Trust. At the death of both spouses, the assets in the B Trust pass free of estate taxes, regardless of the value of the B Trust at that time. The value of the assets in the A Trust is included in the surviving spouse's estate for estate tax purposes, to which the surviving spouse's remaining estate tax exemption amount is applied. The distribution of assets in the B Trust is dictated by the original trust agreement, and the specific terms pertaining to the B Trust cannot be altered, modified, or revoked after the first spouse passes.

A/B/C Trust Planning – A common planning technique used for a family trust when the estate has a value that exceeds the Trustmakers' remaining estate tax exemption amount, and there is additional need for protection of the deceased spouse's assets, such as in blended families. The A Trust and B Trust work the same as in A/B Trust Planning. However, the B Trust is funded with assets up to the value of the deceased spouse's estate tax exemption amount, and any portion of the deceased spouse's half of the estate that exceeds the exemption flows into the "C Trust". This trust may more specifically be referred to as the QTIP or Qualified Terminable Interest Property Trust. At the death of the surviving spouse, the assets in the C Trust are counted with the assets in the A Trust for inclusion in the surviving spouse's estate for estate tax purposes, to which the surviving spouse's remaining estate tax exemption is used. The distribution of assets in the B Trust and C Trust are dictated by the original trust agreement, and the specific terms pertaining to the B Trust and C Trust cannot be altered, modified, or revoked after the first spouse passes.

Administration – The process in which the Trustee, Executor, or Personal Representative collects the decedent's assets, pays the decedent's debts and claims, and distributes the remainder of the estate according to the terms of the trust, Will, or state intestacy rules.

Advance Health Care Directive – A written document that authorizes a named individual to make health care decisions during the incapacity of the person granting the power.

Beneficiary – An individual for whose benefit a Will or trust was created, and who is to receive property by the terms of the Will or trust.

Bypass Trust – A common planning technique used by families for estate tax planning purposes.

Community Property – A form of ownership in California under which property acquired during marriage is presumed to be jointly owned by the spouses.

Decedent – An individual who has died.

Descendant – An individual's children, grandchildren, great-grandchildren, etc.

Distribution – The act of delivering assets to a beneficiary, multiple beneficiaries or a group of beneficiaries either through naming the beneficiary or beneficiaries on title to the assets or titling the assets to a trust for the benefit of the beneficiary or beneficiaries.

Estate Planning – The process by which an individual or individuals design a strategy and execute a trust agreement, a Will, or other documents to provide instructions for the administration of their assets upon their incapacity or death.

Executor – An individual, bank, or trust company that administers and settles the estate of a decedent pursuant to the terms of a Will, or if there was no Will then by the laws of intestacy. May also be referred to as a Personal Representative.

Fiduciary – An individual, bank, or trust company that acts for the benefit of another. Fiduciaries include: Trustees, Executors, and Personal Representatives.

Heir – An individual entitled to a distribution of assets or property interest under applicable state law in the absence of a Will or trust.

HIPAA Authorization – A document that allows the principal to name individuals who will have rights to receive medical information pertaining to the principal

Income – Earnings from principal, such as cash dividends, rent, and interest.

Income Beneficiary – A beneficiary that is to receive income, but not principal, of a trust agreement.

Intestate – When an individual dies without a valid Will or trust, such that the individual's estate is distributed in accordance with the state's intestacy law.

Irrevocable Trust – A trust that cannot be terminated, revoked or otherwise modified or amended by the grantor absent court action.

Issue – An individual's descendants, i.e. children, grandchildren, great-grandchildren, etc.

Personal Liability – A financial obligation for which an individual is responsible, which may be satisfied out of that individual's personal assets.

Pour Over Will – A Will used in combination with a revocable trust to pass title at death to assets or properties that were not transferred to the trust during the Trustmaker's lifetime.

Power of Appointment – A specific power given to a beneficiary under the terms of a trust to appoint property to named individuals upon termination of that beneficiary's interest in the trust, or upon other specified circumstances. This power may be general, allowing the property to be appointed to any individual, or limited, allowing the property to be appointed to a specified group or individuals only.

Power of Attorney for Finances – A written document authorizing one individual to act in another's place as agent or attorney-in-fact with regard to legal and financial matters. The scope of authority granted is specified in the document, and terminates either on the incapacity or death of the individual granting the power.

Principal – Property contributed to a trust to generate income and to be used for the benefit of the named beneficiaries according to the terms of the trust.

Remainder Beneficiary – An individual named to receive an interest in property upon the expiration of an intervening income interest, life estate or term of years.

Self-Dealing – Personally benefiting from a transaction conducted on behalf of a trust or estate.

Successor Trustee – The individual nominated to take the place of the initial Trustee, when the initial Trustee becomes incapacitated, resigns or dies.

Trust - A legal contract/relationship that results when an individual makes a contract/agreement with a Trustee to handle property for the benefit of the beneficiaries. The agreement is normally set out in a written document, which is called the trust instrument, declaration of trust or the trust agreement.

Trustee – An individual, bank, or trust company that holds legal title to property for the benefit of another and acts pursuant to the terms of the trust. An individual can be a Trustee and beneficiary at the same time.

Trustmaker – An individual who transfers property to a Trustee to manage or own subject to the terms of the trust agreement. May also be referred to as a Trustor, Grantor, or Settlor.

ABOUT THE AUTHORS

ROBERT D. VALE, ESQ.

Robert D. Vale is a Partner at McDowall Cotter, APC, with a primary practice in wealth preservation, asset protection and trust and estate administration. This includes working with family businesses on entity formation, succession planning, lease negotiations and other matters particular to family businesses. Robert received his undergraduate degree at the University at California at Davis in 1976, and earned his M.B.A. from the University of Santa Clara in 1979. Robert earned his law degree from the University of the Pacific, McGeorge School of Law, at which he was active in law review and served as president of Phi Delta Phi. He obtained a Masters of Law in Taxation in 2001.

Robert's publications include: *Of Hearts and Minds (Guardians and Trustees); Planning for a Loved One with Special Needs; Planning Strategies for Grandparents; A Will or a Trust, that is the Question.* His awards and recognitions include: William Nagle, Jr. Award for his service to the County Bar Association, Dorothy

Wolf Award for volunteer work with the Legal Aid Society of San Mateo County, and numerous San Mateo County Superior Court Commendations for Service as Judge Pro Tem for Settlement Conferences and Small Claims Appeals.

Robert has been a featured speaker on many occasions and on topics including California real estate, special needs planning, trust administration, planning for pets, basic estate planning and various topics covering advanced estate planning.

BRETT S. LYTLE, ESQ.

Brett S. Lytle is a Partner at McDowall Cotter, APC, where he counsels individuals, families, nonprofits and businesses in legal matters pertaining to estate planning, wealth preservation, and asset protection. Brett received his undergraduate degree in Business Administration from the University of Iowa in 1980. He received a Master's of Science in Taxation and a Jurist Doctorate from the University of Gonzaga in 1984. He then received a Master of Law in Business and Taxation-Transnational Practice from University of the Pacific, McGeorge School of Law in 1985.

Brett is admitted to practice in the California Supreme Court, the District of Columbia Appellate Court, United States Tax Court and United States Court of International Trade. Additionally, he was also a member of the Board of Directors of San Francisco and San Mateo American lung Association, Redwood City AYSO, Mission Hospice, and the Mountain View-Los Altos High School Foundation. In addition, Brett provides a continuing education program entitled "Needs benefit Approach to Estate Planning for Insurance Professionals," and also speaks for charities like the Alzheimer Association, the Northern California Hakka Association, and many more.

STEFANI C. COGGINS, ESQ.

Stefani C. Coggins is an Associate Attorney at McDowall Cotter, APC, with a primary practice in wealth preservation, asset protection and trust and estate administration. Stefani received her Bachelor of Arts degree in Drama from the University of California at Irvine in 2008, and later earned her Juris Doctorate degree and Certificates in Dispute Resolution and International and Comparative Law from Pepperdine University School of Law in 2012. During her time at Pepperdine, Stefani received a CALI Excellence for the Future Award for Interviewing, Counseling, and Planning, and graduated as a member of the Order of the Barristers National Honor Society. Stefani was also active on Pepperdine's Honor's Trial Advocacy Team, and was the 2011 Managing Editor of the *Journal of Business, Entrepreneurship and the Law*. Stefani has published numerous White Papers with McDowall Cotter, APC, with topics ranging from California's Death With Dignity Act to Revocable Transfer on Death Deeds.

In her free time, Stefani is an avid roller derby player, and currently serves as Treasurer and a member of the Board of Directors for Peninsula Roller Girls, Inc., a 501(c)(3) non-profit organization.

This manual is intended only for the purpose of providing general information and does not constitute legal advice. By providing this general information we are not establishing an attorney-client relationship and nothing contained in this manual should be construed to necessarily be applicable to your unique situation. You should always engage the services of an attorney to determine which, if any, legal solutions are right for you.

Made in the USA
Monee, IL
01 April 2021